CREATION AND TIME

a report on the Progressive Creationist book by Hugh Ross

Mark Van Bebber
and
Paul S. Taylor

Eden Productions
2628 West Birchwood Circle
Mesa, Arizona 85202

Published by

Eden Productions (an imprint of Films for Christ)
2628 West Birchwood Circle
Mesa, Arizona 85202
United States of America

Eden Productions is an imprint of Films for Christ, a non-profit, evangelical, interdenominational ministry with an emphasis on apologetics and evangelism — sharing Christ and knowledge of His Creation through the production and distribution of motion pictures, videos and literature. Eden Productions is the book publishing imprint and public school distribution arm of the contributor-supported ministry, Films for Christ.

Cataloging Data

I. Creation and Time: A Report on the Progressive Creationist Book by Hugh Ross / Van Bebber and Taylor

A biblical and theological critique of Progressive Creationist claims made by Hugh Ross of Reasons to Believe in his book, *Creation and Time: A Biblical and Scientific Perspective on the Creation-Date Controversy.*

Includes references and index.

1. Creationism. 2. Bible and science. 3. Science and Faith.

II. Van Bebber, Mark, A. 1961- and Taylor, Paul S., 1953-

Library of Congress Catalog Card Number: 94-61709

Printed and bound in the United States of America

Comments

"This book is not just a rebuttal on *Creation and Time*... it is a bold and courageous attempt to attack the roots of Progressive Creationism... with [its] misguided theology and secular science. This report has taken claim after claim and refuted it on sound theological... grounds. We must view our origins first in the light of the Scriptures because man can so easily distort reality. Christians need to take heed of special revelation that makes it clear that God created heavens and earth in six literal days and that our intelligent and awesome Creator did not need the help of the Big Bang as Hugh Ross promotes to set everything in its place."

D. James Kennedy, D.D., D.Sac.Lit., Ph.D., Litt.D.,
D.Sac.Theol., D. Humane Let. — Chancellor, Knox Theological
Seminary; Senior Minister, Coral Ridge Presbyterian Church;
President, Evangelism Explosion International

"This book is a wake-up call to all Christians, warning us about a serious danger within our midst, the teachings of Hugh Ross. The book leaves the discussion of Dr. Ross's many scientific errors to other writers, and instead it concentrates on his theology. While being graceful and kind to Dr. Ross himself, the authors carefully compare his teachings with those of the Bible, and they clearly point out the very many cases where Dr. Ross's teachings are contrary to a straightforward understanding of Scripture. Every Christian should have this valuable source book for his own protection, because the practical effect of Dr. Ross's teaching is to place a subtle barrier between the believer and the Bible, and between the believer and God Himself."

D. Russell Humphreys, Ph.D. — Physicist and Author

"The teachings of Hugh Ross, including his beliefs in a local Flood and a race of spiritless men and women before Adam and Eve, are really nothing new, but sadly, are permeating through the Christian world... Mark Van Bebber and Paul Taylor, in this comprehensive critique have pointed out the errors of the Ross teachings, and how an acceptance of them undermines the gospel message and the authority of the Word of God. The central argument of the creation movement is not the 'young earth' as such, but that sinful fallible humans, living in a fallen and cursed universe, cannot legitimately use their evolution tainted interpretations of the past to interpret an infallible Word!"

Ken Ham, Dip.Ed. — Director of Creation Science Ministries (USA) and a director of The Creation Science Foundation in Australia and the UK

Contents

*Be diligent to present yourself approved to God,
a worker who does not need to be ashamed,
rightly dividing the word of truth.*

II Timothy 2:15

Introduction

This report examines one of the latest writings of Hugh Ross, *Creation and Time: A Biblical and Scientific Perspective on the Creation-Date Controversy*, published in 1994 by NavPress. The purpose of this report is to document a number of important biblical, theological, language and research errors. Being human, most authors make a certain number of mistakes, and we can certainly understand and overlook normal, run-of-the-mill errors. However, in the case of *Creation and Time* a report now seems necessary. Having followed the author's career for years, it is evident that significant erroneous claims are generally consistent throughout his writings, lectures and video presentations. That is, they are the norm, not the exception. Many of these are so obvious that they should be recognizable as such to any informed Christian, whether old-earther or recent creationist. Dr. Ross has been confronted on these issues by various Christian brothers in person, including ourselves, by phone and by letter, but to little or no avail.

We believe that Dr. Ross is saved, and that his expressed desire to live for Christ is genuine. His desire to evangelize is laudable. It is also good to publicize scientific evidences supporting the existence and power of our Creator. This, and his effort to show people that life could not have been produced by natural processes, in fact, closely parallels our own ministry. We applaud these efforts. We also admire his ability to remain relatively cool and self-controlled under pressure. What distresses us is his continuing use of various erroneous teachings about the Bible. We believe these teachings are leading people down a wrong and dangerous path — a trail trod by many in the past that has repeatedly led ultimately to even more serious theological problems and loss of faith in God's Word.

Please understand that, for the sake of brevity, this report is not meant to be thorough and complete. Many of our notes have been left out to save space. A future publication is planned which will investigate Progressive Creationism in much greater depth and provide a considerably more thorough refutation, both for laypeople and scholars.

Not being astronomers or physicists, we do not deal with Ross's astrophysical claims. We leave that task to those more qualified. It is our understanding that various scientists are currently working on that project.

Unless otherwise indicated, referenced page numbers are from Ross's *Creation and Time: A Biblical and Scientific Perspective on the Creation-Date Controversy.*

Who Is Hugh Ross?

Hugh N. Ross is the president and founder of Reasons to Believe, a Progressive Creationist ministry located in Pasadena, California, which deals with Bible-science and a few other apologetics issues. He received his Ph.D. in astronomy from the University of Toronto. He formerly served the Sierra Madre Congregational Church (Sierra Madre, CA) as Minister of Evangelism. His previous book *The Fingerprint of God* (Orange, CA: Promise Publishing, 1989) made the Christian Booksellers Association's list of Best-Selling Paperbacks.

Dr. Ross is currently the most visible spokesman for Progressive Creationism, a belief which opposes both atheistic evolutionism and historic Christianity's understanding of biblical creationism. The teachings of Progressive Creationism are not new or original to Dr. Ross. However, due to Dr. Ross's efforts, the views of Progressive Creationism have received unprecedented wide and favorable publicity through Christian radio, television and magazines. Because Dr. Ross presents his views as being based on a literal interpretation of the Bible, he has been invited to speak at numerous prominent evangelical churches, schools and ministries. He has a weekly, nationwide television program on (and sponsored by) the Trinity Broadcasting Network (TBN).

Hugh Ross defines Progressive Creationism as *"the hypothesis that God has increased the complexity of life on earth by successive creations of new life forms over billions of years while miraculously changing the earth to accommodate the new life."* [Hugh Ross, "Dinosaurs and Hominids," audiotape (Pasadena, CA: Reasons to Believe, 1990)]

While urging Christians to reject evolutionary theories for the origin of life, he teaches a billions-of-years history beginning with the Big Bang. According to Ross and other Progressive Creationists, Adam and Eve were created from dust after the majority of earth's history had already taken place, including eons of death among the animals. His timeline includes millions of years of major disasters befalling the animals before Adam, including supernovas, asteroid impacts, etc. As a result, animals frequently became extinct, never to be seen by man. Progressive Creationism claims that God stepped in many times to create replacements or improved models — sometimes completely abandoning entire groups of animals, changing the previous course of life on earth. Ross also teaches that the flood of Noah was local, not global.

A brief summary of Dr. Ross's Book

Based on its content, *Creation and Time* could have been titled "Creation in a Great Deal of Time: The Bible and Science Prove It and Young-Earth Creationists are Wrong." The basic purpose of *Creation and Time* appears to be to persuade Christians to accept Progressive Creationism's understanding of the Bible and history. Some of these views include:

- The earth and universe are billions of years old.

- The days of Creation were overlapping periods of millions and billions of years.

- Death and bloodshed have existed from the beginning of Creation and were not the result of Adam's sin. Man was created after the vast majority of earth's history of life and death had already taken place.

- The flood of Noah was local, not global, although it did kill all humans outside the Ark. Earth's geology represents billions of years of history.

To persuade Christians to these viewpoints *Creation and Time* uses the following strategies:

- Claim the moral high ground in the controversy

- Attempt to show that young-earth creationists are misguided fanatics, using bad science, and overblowing the importance of a small issue

- Attempt to show that the Bible allows for long Creation days

- Attempt to show that historic Christianity is in agreement with the notion of non-literal days of Creation and an old-earth

- Attempt to show that young-earth creationism is dangerous to Christianity — making it nearly impossible for many people to accept the Bible and Christ

- Reassure readers that Progressive Creationism is in opposition to evolutionism and atheism.

- Attempt to show that the size of the universe and various other astronomical and physical evidences prove beyond doubt the age of the universe

- Attempt to show that there is no credible scientific evidence for a young earth

---

Under the Progressive Creation scenario,
Christ designed animals to devour each other,
ripping with claws and teeth.
Prior to any connection to man or sin,
He designed these innocent creatures to die this way
by the trillions for millions of years.

- Attempt to show that young-earth creationists are out of touch with reality — worse yet, they are spreading lies and producing hatred against old-earth supporters

- Attempt to show that the discovery of the Big Bang was a wonderful breakthrough for Christianity, pointing to God's existence and the first moment of Creation

- Attempt to show that this long-ages interpretation is the *simplest* reading of the Genesis account

- Attempt to show that the Progressive Creationist interpretation of the Creation "days" agrees beautifully with scientific discoveries — Creation occurred in the exact order that scientists know to be true.

- Attempt to show that the existence of millions of years of death before Adam does not alter the doctrine of atonement or imperil faith and morality.

- Attempt to show that Progressive Creationism is an evangelical position which praises the Creator and is in agreement with most modern Bible scholars who accept the inerrancy of Scripture. To this end, the book prominently displays endorsements from various Christian professors and leaders.

Overall, *Creation and Time* is a general repetition of Ross's earlier books. Various sections have been lifted with little or no change from his previous works. Although there is little new in this presentation, certain refinements and corrections are evident. The book is his most intense attack in writing, to date, on young-earth creationism.

It appears that relatively little of what *Creation and Time* teaches is new or unique to Dr. Ross's ministry. Most Progressive Creationist arguments have been around for decades, many developed more than a century ago. What is new is the unique amount of time and effort being spent. Dr. Ross is devoted full-time to promoting Progressive Creationism, while others had previously been occasional part-time speakers and writers. In addition, Ross and the Reasons to Believe staff have an undeniable flair for successful marketing. As a result, Progressive Creationism is being brought to millions through television, radio, books, lectures and international tours.

A Key Tactic of Progressive Creationism

CLAIM: The age of the earth is "a trivial doctrinal point."

Dr. Ross: *"The battle line has been drawn over a* <u>*peripheral point*</u> — *the age of the universe and our earth."* [p. 9 — emphasis added] *"Misidentifying God or His key attributes could destroy the possibility of a person's relationship with Him. Misunderstanding God's strengths, capacities, and past works can impair the success of such a relationship. But* <u>*misidentifying the timing of God's past works in the cosmos has little or no bearing on that relationship. Nor does it bear upon the Bible's authority*</u>*. It appears ill-advised, then, to make an issue out of such a* <u>*trivial*</u> *doctrinal point."* [p. 11 — emphasis added]

FALSE. Although many Christians miss the connection at first glance, this issue is inseparably linked to the Gospel and the inerrancy of Scripture.

The most successful tactic Progressive Creationists have used to win the hearts and minds of evangelicals is this claim: the age question is a "trivial" and "peripheral" issue — the important thing is that God *is* the Creator, not *when* He did it. Many Christians have thus been misled into believing that the young-earth debate is a side issue and not relevant to everyday Christian life or the salvation message.

As will be shown, the wonderful Good News to mankind about Jesus Christ, our Redeemer and Savior, is foundationally rooted in the Book of Genesis. The origin of death is described in Genesis 2:16-17, 3:1-6 (cf. Romans 5:12; I Corinthians 15:21-22). Death was the promised result of sin. It was also the means by which man would be restored to God. In contrast, Progressive Creationism teaches that death and bloodshed existed long *before* man's existence, contrary to the very message of the Gospel.

Why disbelief in a no-death paradise is not trivial

1. **PHYSICAL DEATH CAME THROUGH SIN** (Genesis 3:19). All people die because of Adam's original sin. Progressive Creationism denies this, saying that animals died for millions of years before Adam and implying that Adam too was doomed to physically die, regardless of sin. For them, death and struggle are a part of life that has existed since the beginning. According to the Progressive Creationist timeline, Adam was, in effect, created on top of a graveyard of decaying or fossilized animals. Almost anywhere he walked, the remains of millions of dead animals were somewhere below his feet — evidence of death and frequent misery on a massive scale. Biblically, physical death is a clear penalty of sin — first demonstrated by the death of the sacrificial animals (beginning with those killed by God to clothe Adam and Eve). This penalty was also verified by the physical deaths of Adam and later, Christ, the perfect sacrifice and atonement.

   - ADAM'S POTENTIAL LIFESPAN. Apparently Adam would never have died if he had not disobeyed (Genesis 2:16-17, 3:22). God expelled Adam and Eve from the Garden and guarded the tree of life so they would not use it to thwart death (Genesis 3:22-23).

   - PAUL'S UNDERSTANDING. The apostle Paul understood the Genesis link, as can be seen in I Corinthians 15, referred to by some as "the definition passage" of the Gospel message. Here, Paul discusses the physical resurrection of Christ and believers. *"For since by a man* [the first Adam] *came death, by a man* [the last Adam] *also came the resurrection of the dead. For as in Adam all die, so also in Christ all shall be made alive"* (I Corinthians

15:21-22, *NASB*). *"Therefore, just as through one man* [the first Adam] *sin entered into the world, and death through sin, and so death spread to all men, because all sinned— ...death reigned from Adam... by the transgression of the one the many died..."* (Romans 5:12,14-15, *NASB*).

- BLOOD SACRIFICE. God's Old Testament requirement for the forgiveness of sins was the physical death of sacrificial animals: *"...without shedding of blood there is no forgiveness"* (Hebrews 9:22, *NASB*). Leviticus 17:11 states *"For the life of a creature is in the blood, and I have given it to you to make atonement for yourselves on the altar; it is the blood that makes atonement for one's life"* (*NIV*).

2. **ORIGINAL PARADISE — or did the perfect, all-knowing, all-powerful God of love create an imperfect Creation?** The Bible certainly suggests that God's creations were fully developed, fully equipped, fully functional, free from disease or suffering. God judged it all as "very good" (Genesis 1:31). In contrast, Progressive Creationism claims that God created a world filled with frequent death, physical and emotional sufferings, cruelties, extinctions, catastrophes and so on — for millions of years. According to Progressive Creationism, when wolves eat lambs and when bears kill baby sea lions, this is exactly the way things were meant to be by God.

   Is this what we should be teaching our children? If so, why has God never revealed this? And why does God refer to a blessed time in the future when the lion will lie down with the lamb? Genesis provides a brief but tantalizing description of the wondrous paradise our Creator lovingly designed. It was far unlike the pain-filled, sin-worn world of degeneration that we experience. There is no biblical reason to believe that the pre-Fall world suffered catastrophes, diseases, parasites, plagues, degenerative mutations, damage of skin and eyes due to the sun's ultraviolet radiation, animals preying on man or animals, etc. Earth began as a paradise, not a world of travail.

3. CORRUPTION AND DECAY OF PARADISE began with man's sin and God's judgment (Genesis 3:14-19).

- DEGENERATED UNIVERSE. Nothing in our fallen world is really perfect today. One day the Creator will burn it all and create a fresh new universe (II Peter 3:10-13, Isaiah 65:17, 66:22). In the original world, all was "very good." It is therefore evident that animals and all creation have degenerated. The Fall and God's curse are the ultimate reasons why our world today is so imperfect — filled with futile problems and suffering. The Flood further caused radical changes in our environment. We are fallen people living in a fallen world.

- THORNS AND THISTLES. Progressive Creationists would be forced to say that thorns and thistles (and all other weeds) did not begin with the Fall, for they are found deep in the fossil record (millions of years before Adam, according to their theory — but buried by the Flood or later, according to young-earth creationism).

- WHAT WERE THE EFFECTS OF SIN? Progressive Creationism contradicts the Bible by limiting the effects to the spiritual death of Adam, exclusion from a non-paradise garden, and a decrease in pain tolerance during childbirth. Essentially, Progressive Creationism teaches that the natural world under Adam's rule remained exactly the same before and after Adam's sin. The world was a rough, tough, grizzly place before Adam sinned. There was death all around, catastrophes, disease, genetic defects, freezing cold, burning heat, etc.

4. **RESTORATION OF PARADISE.** For Christians, there is wonderful hope for the future, an essential part of the ultimate promise of the gospel. One day the Creator is going *"to restore everything, as he promised long ago through his holy prophets"* (Acts 3:21, *NIV*). All things will be restored to the wondrous excellence that He originally created. The world will once again be a paradise.

- PEACEFUL VEGETARIANS. The animals will again be vegetarian and at peace with one another (Isaiah 11:6-7, 9).

- RESTORATION TO WHAT? If Progressive Creationism is true, what kind of world can we look forward to in the restoration? A world of continuing animal death, mutations, extinctions, volcanoes, earthquakes, asteroid impacts, disease, and struggle? The Bible teaches the contrary. We look forward to paradise.

5. **THE PURPOSE OF DEATH.** Why did God send physical death to the world He gave Adam to rule? Many people are frightened of death. Most non-Christians look at the suffering and death in our world and conclude that God must not really be good or loving or even all-powerful. Why would God create a world filled with suffering and death? They fail to see that God created a perfect world, a world free from death. Death is the result of sin, man's rebellion against God. However, in love Jesus Christ (God in the flesh) died in our place and was victorious over death. This is the message of the Gospel!

   - DEATH, A DOOR TO GOD. The final effect of Adam's rebellion might have been eternal separation from God for all humanity. Because of His love, however, God set into motion a plan to one day reunite Himself with man forever. He judged with death, the just penalty for sin, and God used the death of His Son to reconcile the world.

   - JESUS' DEATH AND VICTORY. He then sent His only Son, to become a man like us and to bring us back to Himself. Jesus suffered the Father's penalty of death in His own body. As the only acceptable sacrifice, He shed His spotless, sinless blood to cover the sins of all who would trust in Him. He tasted death for everyone (Hebrews 2:9). He then rose from the dead, demonstrating His power and righteousness. One day he will *put all his enemies under his feet. The last enemy to be destroyed is death*" (I Corinthians 15:25-26, *NIV*).

6. **ANIMAL DEATH.** God originally created a paradise for Adam, free of death and suffering. God placed the curse of death upon the world that Adam ruled, thus animals also

die. The animals became subject to suffering and death along with their master.

- PAUL UNDERSTOOD. Since the Fall, Paul said, *"For we know that the whole creation groans and suffers the pains of childbirth together until now"* (Romans 8:22, *NASB*). Romans 8:19-21 confirms that God's judgment on Adam's sin affected all nature: *"For the anxious longing of the creation waits eagerly for the revealing of the sons of God. For the creation was subjected to futility, not of its own will, but because of Him who subjected it, in hope that the creation itself will be set free from its slavery to corruption into the freedom of the glory of the children of God"* (*NASB*). All creation will rejoice when paradise is returned by its Creator.

- VEGETARIAN "CARNIVORES," ORIGINALLY AND IN THE END. Genesis 1:30 clearly indicates that animals having "the breath of life" did not originally eat other animals. Such behavior was not part of God's original plan for paradise. God told them to eat only plants. The land-dwelling animals and birds were created as vegetarians (Genesis 1:29-30). Predation among these animals did not develop until sometime later in history. It is evident that eventually it will be abolished again (Isaiah 11, 35, 65). Wolves and lions will once again eat plants exclusively.

- MAN ALSO HARMLESS TO ANIMALS. Man was also created to be vegetarian and thus was not meant to kill animals (Genesis 1:29). We were not given permission to eat meat until after the Flood (Genesis 9:2-3), almost two thousand years later.

- LATER FEAR OF MAN. It was not until after the Flood that animals became wary and even terrified of humans. At the unveiling of the rainbow, God put the fear and dread of man into the programmed instincts of animals (Genesis 9:2-3). The reasonable assumption is that they were originally created friendly and trusting of man.

- GRAVEYARD CAME AFTER SIN AND THE FLOOD. In considering the whole of Scripture, it is clear that Adam and Eve were created in a paradise, not a graveyard of dead animals. Because animals did not die until after Adam's sin, the fossils are evidence of death *after* Adam's sin, not before. Because fossilization requires highly unusual circumstances and because most are buried in flood-laid sediments, it seems reasonable to believe that most of these animals were killed and buried by God's global flood judgment in the time of Noah. There are volumes of excellent evidence in support of this belief.

- THE JOYFUL HOPE OF CHRISTIANS. All creatures must now cope with a world that is no longer a paradise. They now struggle to survive in a harsh, fallen, Flood-devastated environment. Will not *all* Creation rejoice when paradise is restored? One day Christ will restore the animals to being vegetarian again. Peace will once again reign.

7. **CHRIST — SADISTIC OR TOTALLY GOOD AND LOVING?** If Christ, the Creator (John 1:1-3, Colossians 1:16, I Corinthians 8:6, Hebrews 1:2), used millions of years of suffering and death to make the animals, how can He be all-loving and all-good? Under the Progressive Creation scenario, Christ designed the animals to devour each other, ripping with claws and teeth. He then further allowed these innocent creatures (with no connection whatsoever to man or sin) to die by the trillions for millions of years due to every catastrophe conceivable. God allowed (or possibly even sent) a multitude of afflictions down on these animals, including diseases of all sorts, plagues, volcanoes, earthquakes, bombardments from outer space, floods, etc. As a result, animals of many types were killed to extinction.

Thus, the Progressive Creation scenario involves a process of elimination, death by fang and claw — cold and unmerciful to the weak. Could even a sadist think of a more cruel and ugly way to produce the animals over which Adam was to rule? What a horrible thing to accuse

Jesus Christ of doing! It is shocking that Progressive Creationism defends this as the process that Jesus set up and ruled till the creation of man. Our Creator's true nature is incompatible with this plan. *God is love!* He sees even the sparrow fall. Animal death came because of man. He said, *"Blessed are the meek"* — not blessed are the strongest and most aggressive.

8. **CHRIST — ALL-POWERFUL, ALL-KNOWING, ABSOLUTE PERFECTION.** If Christ is all of these things, He is certainly capable of creating the world in one blinding instant. Why would such a Creator use a slow process rife with dead ends (repeated animal extinctions) and new starts? Why stretch the process over the lifetimes of millions of generations of animals — all this before ever getting to the point, the creation of man?! The Creator doesn't need time; He doesn't need to experiment. Progressive Creationism stains God's true glory, majesty and power — the very characteristics that define him.

9. **GENESIS IS FOUNDATIONAL.** More Bible writers quoted (or referred to) Genesis than any other book. Both Jesus and Paul quoted from it. Christianity was built upon its foundation. Ultimately, all biblical doctrines of theology are based directly or indirectly on the book of Genesis. If the foundation (Genesis) is damaged, the structure (Christianity) is in peril. Sadly, Progressive Creationists are chiseling away at their own foundations.

10. **TRUST IN GOD'S WORD.** If the Bible is God's Word (as it repeatedly claims), and if Progressive Creationism is true, then God's Word is deceptive. For thousands of years, a literal, straightforward, common-sense reading of Genesis and the rest of Scripture has led millions of intelligent Christians and Jews to believe that: (a) the universe was created in six literal days, (b) the earth is only thousands of years old, (c) animals were not originally carnivores, (d) the earth was created before the stars, (e) the plants were created before the sun, (f) man was created in the beginning (not as the last tiny link in an enormous timeline of earth history), and (g) the Flood was global, not merely local.

- WRONG ALL ALONG? Progressive Creationism contradicts all of these beliefs, and claims it has finally discovered how to correctly interpret Genesis — after thousands of years of misunderstanding. That claim should immediately sound suspicious. If this is true, then one wonders what else Christians have seriously misunderstood.

- GENESIS IS THE FOUNDATIONAL BOOK. If you can't trust Genesis to be literally true and understandable, how can you trust the rest of the Bible? This is why Genesis is the focus of Satan's attack, more than any other book.

- JESUS. Christians should believe Genesis is literally true because Jesus did. God is not a God of deception.

11. **HEALTH OF THE CHURCH.** Rejection of the literal biblical account is adversely affecting the Church. Young-earth creationists are rightly concerned for the long-term health of the Church.

- PATH OF CONFUSION. Many Christians can testify that once they accepted the billions-of-years of secular rationalism they found themselves on a path of increasing confusion and uncertainty about how to interpret Scripture.

- DAMAGE IN THE CHURCH. When uniformitarianism and Darwinism captivated the minds of many in the 1800s, various influential churches and Christian schools began down a road that ended in almost total abandonment of the Christian faith. Their demise began with one small step, which was inevitably followed by another and then another. Eventually, the rest of Genesis was questioned. Soon Abraham was doubted as a historical character, then the Exodus story, the miracles, and then Christ's virgin birth and resurrection.

- SCHOOLS AND SEMINARIES. Because many in church authority have accepted the millions-of-years-of-death-before-Adam scenario, most Christian schools and seminaries have failed to teach the overwhelming evidence for fiat creation and opposing evolutionism. Unfortunately, Christian schools commonly teach theistic evolutionism ("evolution is true, but God made it happen"). Sadly, various teachers who want to stand by the historic belief of the church, recent creation, have been chastised. Many faithful parents have scrimped and saved to send their children to Christian colleges, trusting that they will be properly educated in historic, biblical truths. Tragically, many church-sponsored colleges and seminaries are sowing doubt about God's Word starting on this very issue. As a result, it is all too common to see enthusiastic Christian young people enter seminary or a leading Christian college and then lose their fervor and faith.

- NEXT GENERATION LEADERS. An alarming percentage of the next generation of pastors, Sunday school teachers, lay leaders, and missionaries has been taught that most of the evolutionary theory is acceptable and compatible with Christianity.

- INCREASING LIBERALISM. History has repeatedly shown that Christian colleges and seminaries that accept the millions-of-years-of-death-before-Adam scenario have moved closer and closer to full liberalism over the years, unless strong counteraction is taken.

- Not only are people losing faith in the Bible's accuracy, but the truth of the gospel message is being lost!

Note: Considering the emphasis of Ross's own ministry, it is ironic that he calls the age issue trivial. If so, why has he committed so much time and money to writing and speaking on this very subject? Based upon his own actions, it is doubtful that he really believes this issue is "trivial."

Dual Revelation

The "facts of nature" versus Scripture

Ross: *"On no other issue have the words of the Bible been pitted so sharply against the <u>facts of nature</u>."* [p. 7 — emphasis added] *"We can expect interpretation of the <u>facts of nature</u> to be consistent with the message of Genesis and the rest of canon."* [p. 57 — emphasis added] Throughout *Creation and Time* the pronouncements of current, mainline astrophysics are enthusiastically accepted as fact. Foremost of these is the belief that the distance of the stars and the speed of light prove that the universe is billions of years old.

From the very beginning, *Creation and Time* frames the controversy as revolving around the question of biblical interpretation. It attempts to correct the supposed misinterpretations of Christians who believe the Bible teaches that death began with Adam's sin, not before, and that earth is relatively young.

What is not acknowledged is that many of what Ross purports to be "facts of nature" are actually theories or hypotheses or mere assumptions — human interpretations of nature based on incomplete knowledge.

For Dr. Ross the problem is how to correctly reinterpret the Bible in light of his current list of "facts." In reality, science's understanding of what is a "fact" has changed from decade to decade, especially when it comes to the question of ancient events and origins. Paradigm shifts have occurred again and again. History provides numerous examples.

It is important to remember that:

1. **SCIENCE CANNOT DIRECTLY DEAL WITH THE PAST.** Scientists cannot go back in time for a hands-on examination of events of long ago. Scientists are limited to testing and observing things as they exist now — in the present. We are all impressed with the strides science has made in computer technology, medicine, and space travel. However, we must remember that these are far different subjects than the question of ancient origins. Computer chips and medical inventions exist in the present. Humans can directly observe them. Tests can be confirmed simultaneously in labs throughout the world. However, beliefs about ancient origins are different; they are beyond the reach of finite, mortal humans and therefore involve much hypothesis, assumption and guesswork.

2. **MAJORITY OPINION DOES NOT DETERMINE TRUTH.** Unfortunately, many people seem to be of the opinion that if the majority of scientists believe in something, it must be true. Christians, of all people, should see the clear lie in this thinking. The majority of people have never wanted to accept God's truth. The majority of people did not survive the Flood, either. The Bible says the broad path is the one always followed by the majority. The narrow path is the one which leads to truth and life. The majority of scientists do not believe in most things the Bible says — the miracles, the virgin birth, the global flood, the resurrection, etc. The Bible is true nonetheless. Also remember that most, if not all, important scientific findings were originally minority views.

3. **SCIENTISTS ARE HUMAN.** Many laypeople have a dangerously vaulted view of scientists. Scientists are as human as everyone else. They are fallible, biased and sinful. This affects their theories, their decisions, their research, and their interpretation of evidence. In reality, scientists are not totally objective (especially when it comes to beliefs about origins). Most have a presuppositional belief in the basic tenets of evolution: a billions-of-years-old earth and the interpretation of geology as showing the appearance and progress of animals over eons. Due to this bias, it is very

difficult for them to even consider the existence of evidence to the contrary.

Flushed with the technological advances of our modern age, many have accepted an arrogant view of the extent of human knowledge — and have confused the accomplishments of hard science (testable, replicable) with the potentials of origins science (non-replicable, theory-based). In reality, there is a seemingly infinite amount of knowledge to be learned about the universe. Man has gathered only a tiny fraction of that information. Our understanding of the data is even more limited. Thus, opinions about the distant stars and the ancient past are really very tenuous and change rapidly.

4. **SCIENCE CHANGES**. There is considerable danger in using man's limited scientific knowledge to interpret God's Word. Scientific views continually change. For example, the Big Bang theory is not the first scientific theory to explain the cosmos (and it will not be the last). It was preceded by views that were, in their own day, the consensus of modern science. If we allow current scientific opinion to interpret the Bible for us, we will later need to reinterpret it many times over through coming decades and centuries. Christians should not step on such a slippery slope and risk making a mockery of the Bible.

The belief that astronomy proves a billions-of-years-old universe appears to be the central truth that guides most of Dr. Ross's studies and beliefs. He has shown a great commitment to preaching the "good news" of the Big Bang and a universe which God began to create approximately 17 billion years ago. Ross has found that he cannot simply teach science, his first love. Rather, he must also teach the weaker evidences of the Bible so that he can make his message acceptable to the evangelical community. These points are illustrated in various of his publications, including his audiotape, "Creation Days":

Ross states: *"Why do I take the view that these days of Genesis are long periods of time? Let me again share a little bit about my naive experiences as a young man. You know, I felt that the best arguments for a seventeen or eighteen-billion-year-old universe would come from*

astronomy. I was trained in astronomy and realize that you've got overwhelming evidences in those sciences for that kind of creation date. In fact, that was part of my message, that the evidence in astronomy is so powerful that God created, and created at a definite point in the past, that I use that as a tool for demonstrating that biblical creation was right on target. Part and parcel of that is the billions of years. And I was naive to think, 'Well, of course the Bible addresses this issue, but the scientific data is so much more specific, and is really beyond any real question that that's the way to go.' And so I would try to talk to audiences of Christians and giving the most powerful evidence, namely, the scientific evidence. But what I've discovered is that when you're dealing with... [Christians], they're already, you know, so wrapped up in this single-revelational theology, that this scientific evidence that you're sharing with them is like water off the back of a duck—it doesn't penetrate. So I've taken a different approach. In going into churches, or addressing audiences of Christians, I begin with the biblical evidence. It's not as definitive, it's not as strong, but it's definitive enough, and it's strong enough... Because they consider themselves to be fundamentalists, they're almost obligated to listen to my appeal from Scripture. I'm not talking to you as a scientist. I'm talking to you as a student of the Bible. This is what my study of the Bible has demonstrated. I've found that I can get a whole lot further with that approach than with a straight scientific message."
[Hugh Ross, "Creation Days," audio-tape (Reasons to Believe, 1990)]

CLAIM: Single Revelation is the belief of many young-earth creationists.

Creation and Time accuses many young-earth creationists of holding to a doctrine of single revelation when it says: *"Many young-universe creationists limit the Word of God to the words of the Bible. Since the Bible declares that only God and His Word are truth, these creationists consider information from any source outside the Bible as inferior and suspect."* [p. 55]

FALSE. Few, if any, young-earth creationists believe in a doctrine of single-revelation. In fact, to hold to this doctrine would undermine the very words of Scripture which tell us that God does reveal Himself in creation. If there is such a thing as a young-earth creation scientist who believes in Single Revelation, we have not heard of it in over 25 years in this field and having read most of the creationist literature. The following sections make clear how Progressive Creationists and recent creationists differ in their view of Dual Revelation.

"All Truth is God's Truth"

The battle cry of Progressive Creationism:
Nature is a revelation of God. Since God cannot lie, nature is truth, just as the Bible is truth. Nature is like the sixty-seventh book of the Bible.

How can this charge be answered? Is all truth really God's truth? Yes, indeed it is. However, one must be very careful because man does not always understand or recognize what truth is. As Cervantes said in one of those flashes of wisdom that punctuated the strange doings of Don Quixote, *"Where the truth is, in so far as it is truth, there God is."*

Evangelical theologian Charles Ryrie puts it this way, *"God Himself is the Source of our knowledge of Him. To be sure, all truth is God's truth. But that cliché should be more carefully stated and used than it generally is. Only true truth comes from God, for since sin entered the stream of history man has created that which he calls truth but which is not. Furthermore, he has perverted, blunted, diluted, and corrupted that which was originally true truth that did come from God. For us today the only infallible canon for determining true truth is the written Word of God. Nature, though it does reveal some things about God, is limited and can be misread by mankind. The human mind, though often brilliant in what it can achieve, suffers limitations and darkening."*
Charles Ryrie, *Basic Theology*, p. 25

CLAIM: The facts of nature are like a 67th book of the Bible.

"God's revelation is not limited exclusively to the Bible's words. The facts of nature may be likened to a sixty-seventh book of the Bible... Some readers might fear I am implying that God's revelation through nature is somehow on an equal footing with His revelation through the words of the Bible. Let me simply state that truth, by definition, is information that is perfectly free of contradiction and error. Just as it is absurd to speak of some entity as more perfect than another, so also one revelation of God's truth cannot be held as inferior or superior to another." [pp. 56-57]

MISLEADING AND FALSE. Progressive Creationism's "facts of nature" should not be likened to a 67th book of the Bible. To do so indicates an inaccurate understanding of nature's revelation to humanity.

1. NO AUDIBLE VOICE. Psalm 19:3 confirms that general revelation, *"the revelation of God's glory through the heavens is... wordless and inaudible."* [Bruce A. Demarest, "General Revelation," in Walter A. Elwell, editor, *Evangelical Dictionary of Theology* (Grand Rapids, MI: Baker Book House, 1984), p. 945] David praises God for His general and special revelation. Psalm 19:1-6 depicts the message, manner and extent of nature's revelation. The first part affirms that nature (specifically the heavens) testifies, by its very existence, to God's glory. The last portion testifies to its worldwide scope. The middle part shows, when translated literally, that the message of God's glory is proclaimed in silence. Bible students should note that many translations of this section erroneously give the opposite impression. Translations such as the *NIV* and *NJKV* followed the *King James Version's* example and added words *not* in the original text. (Italic words in the KJV are not found in the Hebrew text.) Unfortunately, the additions changed the meaning to the opposite of the original intention. The *Word Biblical Commentary* correctly translates verse 3 as follows: *"There is no speech and there are no words; their voice is inaudible."* [Peter C. Craigie, *Word Biblical Commentary, Psalms 1-50* (Waco, TX: Word Publishers, 1983), p. 179]

Nature, without revealing specific truths about God, is a constant reminder to the glory of the Creator. The truths presented in the first 6 verses of Psalm 19 are of a general nature and add little to one's knowledge of God or the world. It is interesting to note the word David uses for God in these verses: "El," the general Hebrew word for deity. In verses 7-14, David praises God for His special revelation to mankind, the words of the Bible. Each of David's praises are very specific as he reflects on the truths gained through the law. In this section, David uses God's personal name, "Yahweh." Thus, David demonstrates the differences in God's special and general revelations. While nature reveals God as creator, it is only through the Bible that one learns to have a relationship with Him.

*See to it that no one takes you captive
through philosophy and empty deception,
according to the tradition of men,
according to the elementary principles of the world,
rather than according to Christ.*

Colossians 2:8

Nature's message is general, yet even without words the heavens declare God's glory. Mankind is certainly able to discern some things about God from nature (His existence, invisible attributes and eternal power — Romans 1:20), but the fact that nature has no speech or voice limits its ability to be specific. This is particularly true when it comes to the ancient past or distant future. Fossils and rocks don't come with date labels and photographs of the living animals attached. Unlike the Bible, the "message" of the "book" of nature is not written or spoken.

2. SUBJECT TO HUMAN INTERPRETATION. Although nature is exceedingly dramatic in the presentation of God's revelation, it is subject to human interpretation. Nature contains an enormous amount of information, but man is

probably incapable of clearly and reliably evaluating its subtleties when it comes to theology, beyond understanding the basic revelation of God's existence and character. On many matters, it is naive, and exceedingly dangerous to rate sinful man's incomplete and changing understanding of this degenerating universe as equal in clarity with the written Word of God! Such views have led to dreadful errors. The Bible has demonstrated its beautiful accuracy again and again, in contrast to the "scientific" pronouncements of humans which have frequently been wrong and often dominated by blinding bias.

Some have objected, "Yes, nature is subject to human interpretation, but so is the Bible." Although we must always take great care in our interpretation of the Bible, there are several reasons why we must base our understanding of the world upon the objective truths presented in the specific Word of God.

3. WRITTEN WORDS. The written revelation of God is communicated by means of words. Verbal communication is subject to the rules of grammar, context, and culture and is therefore open to objective, hermeneutic study. Nature, on the other hand, is the revelation of God in general fashion and is subjective in nature (see above). The words of the Bible do not change, while man's environment (nature) and understanding continually change (see section below).

4. LIMITED REVELATION IN NATURE. While it is true that the revelation that God intended in nature is surely understood (and therefore man is without excuse), the Bible explains that the revelation of nature is limited to demonstrating God's existence and power.

5. CLARITY. The vast majority of the Bible is quite clear and relatively easy to understand. Christian Reformers of the 16th century proclaimed *"total confidence in what they called the perspicuity of Scripture... the clarity of Scripture. They maintained that the Bible is basically clear and lucid. It is simple enough for any literate person to understand its basic message. ...Luther, for example, was convinced that what was obscure and difficult in one part of Scripture was stated more clearly and*

simply in other parts of Scripture. ...What kind of God would reveal his love and redemption in terms so technical and concepts so profound that only an elite corps of professional scholars could understand them? ...Biblical Christianity is not an esoteric religion. Its content is not concealed in vague symbols that require some sort of special 'insight' to grasp. There is no special intellectual prowess or pneumatic gift that is necessary to understand the basic message of Scripture. ... The Bible speaks of God in meaningful patterns of speech. Some of those patterns may be more difficult than others, but they are not meant to be nonsense statements that only a guru can fathom." [R.C. Sproul, *Knowing Scripture* (Downers Grove, IL: InterVarsity Press, 1977), p. 15-17] Josh McDowell affirms, *"The message of the Bible is clear for those who will read it and seek to find out its meaning. The problem comes when people bring their preconceived notions to the Bible and attempt to make the Word fit their ideas. This is not the fault of the Bible, but of the persons who force the Bible to say what they want it to say."* [Josh McDowell and Bill Wilson, *A Ready Defense* (San Bernardino, CA: Here's Life Publishers, Inc., 1990, p. 180]

6. STABILITY. The major, theological interpretations (i.e., Creation, Redemption, etc.) of God's Word have remained relatively unchanged while the "facts" of science change often. The theologian who feels that he has discovered something new in the Scriptures, something never properly understood in previous generations, is wise to rethink his position. On the other hand, there have been great changes in what is considered "scientific fact" over just the last few hundred years. The scientific "truths" of "yesterday" are denounced "today" and ridiculed "tomorrow."

7. CONTAMINATION BY EVOLUTIONISM. Profound shifts have occurred due to the popularity of Darwinism. Evolution has become the foundation of many of the theories pronounced as "facts" by modern science.

8. HUMAN PERVERSION. Just as sinful mankind has endlessly attempted to pervert the Church's interpretation of Scripture, man has also attempted to pervert its interpretation of the message of nature. God intended nature to reveal His existence and power. Man has perverted science (through evolutionism and other errors) and has attempted

to demonstrate that God does not exist or that His power is limited.

When all of these factors are considered, Christians are well advised to place their trust upon the specific revelation of God's word. This certainly does not imply that Christians should avoid the fields of science, but rather that all Christians, whether scientists or shoe salesmen, need to continually examine whether their worldview is truly Bible centered.

9. NATURE HAS DEGENERATED. Nature, and thus God's revelation in nature, has degenerated from its original perfection. The Bible tells us specifically about two occasions in which earth has been terribly affected; the fall of mankind and the global flood of Noah. It is apparent that Dr. Ross's understanding of how sin affected the world is not in line with God's Word. He acknowledges almost no physical effects in nature caused by the Fall. Nor does he have a clear biblical understanding of the effects of the Flood. He and many other Progressive Creationists believe Noah's Flood had no significant effect on earth's geology. They believe the Flood was local, limited to the plains of Mesopotamia.

Dr. Ross believes that the earth was created approximately 4.5 billion years ago and has undergone continual change ever since, including millions of years of death, extinction and suffering. Therefore, the thought of a true original paradise is foreign to his theological system. He simply acknowledges that there was a garden area God made especially nice for Adam and Eve, people did live to great ages, and Adam did walk with God.

Creation and Time states, *"While the sin we human beings commit causes us all naturally to react negatively to <u>decay, work, physical death, pain, and suffering</u>, ...there is <u>nothing</u> in Scripture that compels us to conclude that none of these entities existed before Adam's first act of rebellion against God."* [p. 69 — emphasis added]

In fact, the Bible does teach very specifically that the entire creation has been affected by man's sin. The whole creation has been made ineffective, causing it to groan as it awaits its free-dom from its bondage to sin and decay (Romans 8:19-21). Animals were not created carnivorous, for God commanded that they eat only plants (Genesis 1:29-30). Death (physical and spiritual) entered the world through Adam's sin (Genesis 2:17, 3:19; Romans 5:12, 6:23; I Corinthians. 15:20-23). Although work and pain existed before sin, they were greatly increased after the fall (Genesis 3:16-19). Clearly, the Bible tells us that the world that we are familiar with is very different from the one which God created and pronounced as "very good." It was a world without sin and suffering, without thorns and thistles and without the oppression we witness all around us today. How then, in light of such strong biblical evidence can Dr. Ross ask the following question?

Concerning the pre-Fall world, *Creation and Time* asks, *"Were con-ditions significantly different in the past?"* [p. 88] Dr. Ross claims that our planet has always been subject to catastrophes and violent preda-tion. He says that billions of years before Adam, there were superno-vas and collisions with meteorites that wiped out millions of animals and caused "mass extinction." There were floods, hurricanes, torna-does, harmful mutations and diseases of all sorts. In other words, God used "random, wasteful, inefficiencies" to create the world into which Adam was placed. [*Creation and Time*, pp. 65-69, 88; Hugh Ross, "Species Development: Natural Process or Divine Action," audiotape, tape 2, side 1 (Pasadena, CA: Reasons to Be-lieve, 1990)]

How can a legitimate, biblical concept of Creation be built upon a cracked foundation, marred with inconsistencies? Ross has constructed his ministry upon beliefs that are incompatible with the plain-literal sense of Scripture (death and suffering before Adam, a billions-of-years chronology, a local Flood, a lack of understanding of the terrible effect of sin on the earth, and a naively-high view of nature's revelation vs. God's Word).

Nature certainly does not possess the ability to clearly teach other matters of doctrine on a basis of equal authority as the written word of God and should not be likened to a 67th book of the Bible.

According to *Creation and Time*, neither is inferior or superior to the other, they are simply *"different, just like the content of Ezra is distinct from that of Romans."* [p. 57]

As we have seen, however, for mankind this equality is not valid. For fallen, finite humans the Bible is clearly superior to the revelation of nature when it comes to ancient history, an explanation of the gospel, a description of Creation, the Flood judgment, etc. Nature provides information about the _general_ message that there is a God and that He is a powerful Creator. The Bible tells us in _specific_ words the details of Creation and redemption. Man's biased, incomplete, prideful, changing and fallible interpretations of nature and ancient events must never be given greater authority than the clear words of God.

CLAIM: Observation of the universe (general revelation) is sufficient to discover the gospel.

Dr. Ross apparently believes that knowledge gained through the observation of the universe is sufficient to gain salvation and Christian maturity. For example, his previous book claimed that *"the plan of salvation as stated in the Bible can be seen through observation of the universe around us. Thus, all human beings have a chance to discover it. The Bible is the only one of all religious writings which declares a message in full agreement with (and, of course, amplification of) the gospel message seen in creation."* [The Fingerprint of God, p. 179]

"The Bible includes an account of an ancient character, Job (Job 7-19), who without the aid of Scriptures, and in opposition to the religion of his peers, discerned all the elements of 'the gospel,' the good news of how man can find eternal life in God." [The Fingerprint of God, p. 181 — emphasis added]

"The creation, thus, reveals all the necessary steps to develop a right relationship with God. These steps are uniquely corroborated by the Bible." [The Fingerprint of God, p. 182 — emphasis added]

Creation and Time also states, *"in addition to the words of the Bible being 'God-breathed, ...useful for teaching, rebuking, correcting, and training in righteousness' (II Timothy 3:16), so also are the words of God spoken through the work of His hands."* [p. 56 — emphasis added]

FALSE. Nature does not communicate the whole gospel. Strong says, *"The Scriptures plainly declare that the revelation of God in nature does not supply all of the knowledge which a sinner needs (Acts 17:23; Ephesians 3:9)."* [Augustus H. Strong, *Systematic Theology* (Valley Forge, PA: Judson Press, 1907), p. 27] Theologian Bruce Demarest calls such a view "extreme" and "liberal." Authorities such as Augustine, Luther, Calvin, Hodge, Warfield, Henry and others also disagree with Ross's position. [Bruce A. Demarest, "General Revelation," in Walter A. Elwell, editor, *Evangelical Dictionary of Theology* (Grand Rapids, MI: Baker Book House, 1984), p. 944]

Most Christians accept the reality of Dual Revelation (God has revealed Himself both through nature and Scripture). However, theologians note that the revelation of nature (usually called General Revelation) is limited and is not as specific as the Bible; God's <u>words</u> to humanity.

Dr. Ross does not seem to recognize this limitation. In fact he lists 23 verses which he claims as support for his view that nature is *"likened to a sixty-seventh book of the Bible."* [p. 56] It should be noted that even the verses he lists acknowledge the limited nature of general revelation. These Scriptures teach that nature reveals God's existence, glory, power, righteousness, wisdom, and kindness. Actually, it is a long stretch to suggest that several of these verses mention nature's general revelation at all (*See:* Job 10:8-14, 34:14-15, 35:10-12; Psalm 85:11, 98:2-3; Romans 2:14-15; Colossians 1:23).

Two of the verses referred to by Ross are particularly interesting, as they contradict his view. Ecclesiastes 3:11 confirms that although God has revealed himself to humanity in nature, *"yet they cannot fathom what God has done from beginning to end"* (*NIV*). Romans 10:14-18 clearly teaches that although man receives general revelation about the existence and glory of God (quote from Psalm 19:1-4), *"How then shall they call upon Him in whom they have not believed? And how shall they believe in Him whom they have not heard? And how shall they hear without a preacher? ...So faith comes from hearing, and hearing by the word of Christ"* (*NASB*). Scripture is clear that the gospel which saves and sanctifies is found only in the words of the Bible.

Another New Testament passage which Dr. Ross uses to support his view that the gospel of Jesus Christ may be found in nature is Colossians 1:23. Dr. Ross writes, *"Colossians 1:23 states that <u>salvation</u> 'has been proclaimed to every creature under heaven.'"* (p. 56 — emphasis added) He teaches that this verse makes it clear that the gospel of salvation has been revealed by means of God's revelation in the heavens.

FALSE. This is another serious scriptural error.

Colossians 1:23b says, *"This is the gospel that you heard and that has been proclaimed in all creation under heaven, and of which I, Paul, was made a minister"* (*NASB*). Dr. Ross claims this verse means that everyone can know the gospel of God through His revelation in the heavens. This is a serious misunderstanding of this verse.

1. The gospel, as contextually described by Paul in Colossians chapter 1, contains in-depth information about Jesus Christ, the Creator/Sustainer/Redeemer of mankind. Certainly, the revelation of nature cannot communicate such a precise message.

2. The phrase *"to every creature"* states the object of the preaching and is modified by the phrase *"under heaven,"* which emphasizes the universal scope of the gospel (just what is expected according to Christ's own words in Mark 16:15, Matthew 28:18-20 and Acts 1:8). Paul's message of the universal, genuine gospel is an important foundation for the verses which follow, describing the mystery of the Jewish/Gentile union in Christ (Colossians 1:24-29).

3. Further contextual proof that Paul emphasized the <u>extent</u> of the spread of the gospel rather than the <u>mode</u> of revelation is seen in Colossians 1:5-6 which states, *"because of the hope laid up for you in heaven, of which <u>you previously heard in the word of truth, the gospel, which has come to you, just as in all the world</u> also it is constantly bearing fruit and increasing"* (*NASB*). Thus, Paul states that the faith which is increasing in the

Colossian church was brought in the same manner as throughout the world. Verse 7 tells us the means of this communication of the gospel, *"just as you learned it from Epaphras, our beloved fellow bond-servant..." (NASB).*

It is clear from the context and message of the gospel that Paul never intended to communicate the false idea that nature could proclaim the gospel of salvation. Dr. Ross is terribly incorrect in taking this unorthodox view concerning nature's revelation to mankind. Rather than providing a revelation sufficient for salvation, *"general revelation serves only to condemn the sinner and to establish his guilt-worthiness before God (Rom. 1:20)."* [Bruce A. Demarest, "General Revelation," in Walter A. Elwell, editor, *Evangelical Dictionary of Theology* (Grand Rapids, MI: Baker Book House, 1984), p. 945]

CLAIM: The universe is billions of years old.

In reading *Creation and Time* and Dr. Ross's other works, it becomes apparent that the central belief of much of his teachings is this: the universe is billions of years old and astronomy proves it. Again and again Dr. Ross makes claims for a billions-of-years-old universe. He and other Progressive Creationists fervently believe that the size of the universe and various other astronomical discoveries prove this beyond any doubt. Ross rejects as nonsense all suggestions from science that earth and the universe could be young. [*Creation and Time*; Hugh Ross, *The Fingerprint of God*, second edition (Promise Publishing Co., 1991); etc.]

Ross emphasizes man's place in this vast timeline, *"If the time since the creation of the universe were scaled down to a single year, the whole of human history would be less than one minute."* [Hugh Ross, *The Fingerprint of God*, p. 178 — emphasis added, also see pp. 159-160]

FALSE. The Scriptures contradict such a teaching. Also, not all scientific evidences lead to the conclusion that the universe is billions of years old. Nor does the universe's vastness necessarily mean that it is of great age.

The simple fact is, the only one who has observed the entire history of the universe from beginning to end is God. Obviously, no scientist was there billions of years ago, nor can anyone go back in a time machine to make critical measurements and tests. Only the Creator is in a position to know with certainty the true history and age of the universe. Man's finite powers of observation and sin-polluted, degenerate minds are simply not capable of knowing many absolute facts about the ancient past.

What we do have is a witness, however. His Word to humanity is clear. The Bible indicates that all Creation was completed during six days (evidently six earth rotations). It is widely agreed that the biblical genealogies carefully provide a line of descent from the first Adam to the second Adam. This genealogy provides a good general indication of the elapsed time. Some scholars argue that there may be some "gaps" in the genealogies. That is, rather than reporting a father/son relationship, a portion may record a grandfather/grandson or even great-grandfather/great-grandson relationship. However, even if this is true, it would be absurd to accept insertions of tens of thousands of years in the genealogies.

New scientific theories exist which explain the size of the universe in agreement with the biblical timescale. One example is the young-earth relativistic cosmology formulated by physicist Dr. Russell Humphreys based on Einstein's general theory of relativity. We are told that this alternative to the "Big Bang" has been well-received by scientists trained in relativity. [See: D. Russell Humphreys, Starlight and Time (Colorado Springs, CO: Master Books, 1994)] In addition, the majority of scientific age estimation methods indicate a young earth. [See: Paul S. Taylor, The Illustrated ORIGINS Answer Book (Mesa, Arizona: Eden Productions, 1992) and Dr. John D. Morris, The Young Earth (Colorado Springs, CO: Master Books, 1994)] Dr. Ross's bias is apparent in his willingness to accept only those scientific methods that agree with his belief in billions of years. In the final analysis, none of man's scientific age estimation methods can be considered foolproof, young or old. Views that reigned for decades have often been quickly discarded upon the discovery of unexpected, new evidence or upon finding a new way of looking at an old question. We would prefer to stick with the testimony of the only eyewitness to those ancient events, God.

Other Theological Considerations

CLAIM: God created many carnivorous animals in the beginning — long before Adam's sin.

Dr. Ross does not believe the Garden of Eden was free of death, pain, suffering or degeneration — a world created in perfection. He explains at length the nature of the food chain, suggesting that carnivorous activities are essential and beneficial, having originated at God's command from the very beginning. Ross explains that people often don't understand the importance of the food chain and incorrectly label it as evil and emotionally offensive. *Creation and Time* states, *"Again, I am not disputing that God could have done things differently. But our job as thinking people, whether scientists or theologians, is not to question God's motives or His ways but rather to determine what, in fact, He has done and is doing."* [pp. 63, 64]

> FALSE. It is significant that Dr. Ross fails to quote from the Bible passage which most directly sheds light on this issue. Genesis 1:29-30 tell us, *"And God said, 'See, I have given you every herb that yields seed which is on the face of all the earth, and every tree whose fruit yields seed; to you it shall be for food. Also, to every beast of the earth, to every bird of the air, and to everything that creeps on the earth, in which there is life, I have given every green herb for food'; and it was so"* (NKJV). Thus, in the original creation, God intended that animals and humans eat a vegetarian diet. All that had "the breath of life" were created as plant-eaters, not carnivores. Because of sin, God cursed the ground and physical creation (Genesis 3:17). Scripture says the whole creation has been affected, causing it to groan as it awaits free-

dom from bondage to decay (Romans 8:20-22). The global Flood judgment changed earth even more (Genesis 8:21).

It is true that we don't have all the specific answers about what the world was like before the Fall. There are many legitimate questions regarding this aspect of creationism. More research is definitely needed (an interesting analysis of this topic can be found in chapter 6 of the *The Answers Book* published by Master Books and Creation Science Foundation). The Bible is clear, however, that the animals in God's original creation were not carnivorous. As Christians, we look forward to the time when Christ will restore much of the original order of things. One day God will restore paradise. Once again the lion will lie down with the lamb and eat straw like the ox (Isaiah 11, 35, 65). Clearly, the world we now see is drastically different from the world God presented to Adam.

Responding to Dr. Henry Morris's claim that a good, loving and merciful God would not create the world through billions of years of death, pain and suffering (all prior to man's original sin), Ross states, *"If these assertions are true, what can we say of the present era? God could do much right now to reduce our suffering. But a loving, merciful God allows the epitome of His creation — mankind — to suffer discomfort, illness, injury, and death. God even calls the death of His saints precious (Psalm 116:15)."* [p. 88]

DEATH, AN ENEMY. Currently, in the post-Fall world, God does allow suffering and death, but we should not suppose that God takes pleasure in our suffering or death. In fact, John 11:33 (in the original language) demonstrates that Jesus' feelings toward death are of indignation and agitation. Although death is a doorway to God, it is also man's enemy — an enemy defeated by Christ's resurrection (I Corinthians 15:51f).

PSALM 116:15. Ross seems to misunderstand Psalm 116:15. In reading the context and Hebrew wording, it becomes clear that the death of one of God's chosen is very costly to Him. Death is not precious to God, if by that one means that He delights in the death of His saints.

THE PROBLEM OF PAIN AND SUFFERING. Furthermore, it is Progressive Creationism, not young-earth creationism, that causes a problem on the subject of pain and suffering. Anyone who is active in evangelism knows that the issue of pain and suffering is a frequent obstacle in many people's minds. People blame God for it, and question the claim of Christianity that God is "love." Their argument becomes more valid under the Progressive Creationist position. According to Ross, for the most part, the world we experience really is the way God made things. Death, disease, catastrophes, extinctions, and a multitude of physical suffering came from God, woven throughout the design of nature from the very beginning. Sinless man was placed into this situation from the beginning!

- THE IMPLICATION. Modern secular thinkers are quick to see the implication and want nothing to do with such a God, for the *"process is rife with happenstance, contingency, incredible waste, death, pain, and horror. ...the God implied by evolutionary theory and the data of natural history ...is not a loving God who cares about His productions. He is ...careless, indifferent, almost diabolical. He is certainly not the sort of God to whom anyone would be inclined to pray."* [David L. Hull, "The God of the Galapagos," *Nature*, Vol. 352 (August 8, 1992), p. 486]

Little more than five thousand years have passed since the creation of the universe...

John Calvin

- THE BIBLICAL ANSWER. In contrast, the answer of the Bible is much more satisfying to those who seek answers on the topic of pain and suffering. The biblical answer can briefly be summarized thusly:

   Our pure, holy, loving Creator created a paradise for us, designed for our enjoyment. Man had every opportunity to enjoy that perfect world forever. Instead, Adam and Eve rebelled. This sin corrupted their souls and bodies and all paradise — cutting them off from close communion with their holy Creator. Our loving and just God did not choose to destroy them forever. Instead, He immediately set into motion a plan of sacrificial redemption. He provided death, both as a judgment and a blessing, a means of ultimately restoring man to Himself. As a natural result and as a judgment of Adam's sin, death and suffering came upon all the world man ruled and upon all of Adam's descendants. The suffering we experience is the result of human sin; this is not the way God originally wanted things to be. When the perfect time was come, God sacrificed His Son to redeem man and conquer death forever. Ultimately, he will restore paradise! Again there will be no death, no suffering, no evil. Our experience in this world of hardship and travail will be but a brief moment in a wondrous eternity.

CLAIM: Plants were killed before Adam's sin, so there clearly was death before the Fall.

Creation and Time tries to persuade the reader that death before Adam's sin is a huge problem for young-earth creationists. The book explains that *"many species of life cannot survive for even three hours without food, and the mere ingestion of food by animals requires death of at least plants or plant parts."* [p. 61] It also states, *"The destruction (large plant eating animals) wreak on their environment in attempting to devour sufficient calories results in the death of many plants and smaller animals, arguably more death than is caused by large carnivores... But even plants suffer when they are eaten. They experience bleeding, bruising, scarring, and death. Why is the suffering of plants acceptable and not that of animals?"* [p. 63]

FALSE. Who really believes that plants suffer — perhaps people who think they must talk to their plants or people that hug trees? Certainly animal rights groups don't protest the mowing of lawns or pruning of trees. There is no evidence that plants have minds or self-consciousness. They don't have brains by which they are able to interpret nerve or tissue damage as "pain." From a biblical point of view, they are evidently not alive in the same sense as humans and animals. The Word of God makes a theological distinction between the life of animate beings (animals and man) and plants.

We have found no instance where Scripture attributes life to plants. The Hebrew word "nephesh" is one of the most commonly used words for life. It is never used in connection with plants. Plants are never said to contain "the breath of life,"("chay" or "chayyah") or "spirit" ("ruwach"). The Bible certainly never speaks of plants as having minds or emotions. The Bible tells us that the life of a creature is in the blood (Leviticus 17:11-14). Plants do not have a true blood system. Plants are not classified as having muscle and flesh ("basar"), as are animals and men.

In the parable of the sower and the seed, the plants on rocky ground "withered." The same happened when Jesus cursed the unfruitful fig tree. Evidently they shriveled and ceased to exist. But in neither case does Scripture refer to the plants as having "died" or having been "killed." Although, in modern, scientific terminology, plants are known as "living" organisms (i.e., growing and reproducing), the Bible does not classify them as such. Plants are not "alive" in a biblical sense. None of the biblical words associated with living beings are ever used in the context of plants in Scripture. In other words, plants should not be biblically classified as "living" in the sense used in *Creation and Time*. This smokescreen argument should divert no one from the heart of the matter: God created a wonderful paradise without death, suffering, oppression and bloodshed.

CLAIM: Nowhere does the Bible say that animal death did not exist before the Fall.

Creation and Time claims that death in the animal kingdom could have existed before the fall because the Scriptures tell us that only man was affected by death through sin. *"Of all life on the earth, only humans have earned the title 'sinner.' Only humans can experience 'death through sin.' Note that the death Adam experienced is carefully qualified in the text as being visited on 'all men' - not on plants and animals, just on human beings (Romans 5:12,18-19)."* [p. 61]

FALSE. The Bible does indicate that animal death resulted from Adam's sin.

Romans 5:12 states, *"Therefore, just as through one man sin entered into the world, and death through sin, and so death spread to all men, because all sinned—"* (*NASB*). From this verse we learn that sin and death are interwoven. We also note that sin entered into the world; it had a universal effect. True, this verse does emphasize the effect of sin and death upon men, but it does not preclude death from the animal kingdom. *"Sin entered into the world"* could refer only to the world of men (as Dr. Ross suggests), or it could refer to all creation. The context does not directly address this question. It seems likely, however, that since other passages of Scripture tell of sin's effect upon nature that this is the intended meaning here as well.

> *All Christians, whether scientists or shoe salesmen,*
> *need to continually examine whether*
> *their worldview is truly Bible centered.*

Romans 8:19-22 demonstrates that, due to sin, God subjected creation to futility. This subjection is first referred to in Genesis 3:14-19. The serpent is condemned to a more severe curse than all the other animals on the face of the earth. The physical earth is also affected, *"Cursed is the ground because of you... thorns and thistles it shall grow for you"* (Genesis 3:17,18, *NASB*). Indeed, we notice that prior to the Fall all creatures that have "the breath of life" ate only plants (Genesis 1:30). The Bible also speaks of a future restoration of nature — Isaiah 65:25 and Acts 3:21. Much of creation will be restored to its condition before sin, the curse, and the Flood. Surely, these verses show that sin and death have affected the world and not simply mankind.

Note also that man was given headship over all creation. Therefore, his sins and God's judgment would naturally affect the world. Certainly this truth is also emphasized in the account of the Genesis flood. God brought judgment against all the animals, the earth and humanity because of sin.

Does it sound strange for Paul to state that death entered the world because of man's sin? No, this is the clear and harmonious teaching of Scripture. Dr. Ross's belief that only man is affected by the sins of humanity is without biblical support.

CLAIM: The death that came through sin was spiritual, not physical.

Creation and Time uses one more argument to show that Romans 5:12f does not require a pre-Fall world without death. Ross reasons that the death resulting from sin is spiritual, not physical, and therefore, that this verse has no real bearing on the state of the original creation. He further claims that both Genesis and I Corinthians 15 support the view that spiritual death is the penalty for sin. [p. 61]

FALSE. Once again, the Bible disagrees with the teachings of Progressive Creationism. Romans 5:12 may be speaking of the *united* penalty for sin — physical and spiritual death. Physical death is certainly a consideration of these verses. Romans 5:14 states, *"Death reigned from Adam until Moses, even over those who had not sinned in the likeness of the offense of Adam, who is a type of Him who was to come"* (NASB). Clearly, Paul teaches that the existence of physical death (prior to the giving of the law) demonstrated humanity's sinfulness. Perhaps this is why the phrase, *"and he died"* is repeated over and over again throughout the genealogy of Genesis chapter 5, a confirmation that sin has brought the unnatural state of death into our world.

Lest there be any mistake about what God meant when He said that Adam would die, God declared to Adam, *"By the sweat of your face you shall eat bread, till you return to the ground, because from it you were taken; for you are dust, and to dust you shall return"* (Genesis 3:19, NASB). God then guarded the tree of life with an angel. This strong measure prevented Adam and Eve from eating its fruit and avoiding physical death (one of the wages of sin).

Dr. Ross's wrong view of death's origin is not new. The same belief can be traced back to the monk Pelagius around 400 A.D. As the scholar Millard Erickson explains, *"The Pelagian view... is that man was created mortal. Just as everything about us dies sooner or later, so it is and has always been with man. The principle of death and decay is a part of the whole creation. The Pelagians point out that if the Calvinist view is correct, then it was the serpent who was right and Jehovah was wrong in saying, 'In the day that you eat of it you shall die,' for Adam and Eve were not struck dead on the day of their sin. Physical death, in the Pelagian view, is a natural accompaniment of being human. The biblical references to death as a consequence of sin are understood as references to spiritual death, separation from God, rather than physical death."* [Millard J. Erickson, *Christian Theology* (Grand Rapids, MI: Baker Book House, 1985), pp. 611-612] Largely due to the efforts of Augustine, Pelagius was rightly denounced by the early church for his views and for the heretical beliefs that he derived from them.

Creation and Time similarly attempts to use Genesis 2:17, "When Adam sinned, he instantly 'died' just as God said he would ('In the day that you eat of it, you shall surely die' - Genesis 2:17, NKJV). Yet, he remained alive physically and soulishly... He died <u>spiritually</u>." [p. 61 — emphasis added]

Here is an inconsistency. *Creation and Time* points to God's warning, "*<u>In the day</u> that you eat of it, you shall surely die*" (Genesis 2:17, *NKJV*). On what basis does Ross require that "day" ("yom") in this context means a normal, 24 hour day when the word is used without "morning and evening" and without an ordinal modifier? Why should not this use of "yom" be interpreted as an unspecified period of time, as Ross advocates for the previous uses? In other words, if Dr. Ross were consistent in his teachings, "day" in this verse would not require immediate death, physically or spiritually.

"Yom" certainly can be used to mean something other than 24 hours. For example, in English one might read, "In George Washington's <u>day</u> men wore powdered wigs." It is reasonable to assume that the use of "yom" in Genesis 2:17 may communicate something other than a 24-hour day. Yom is used similarly in other parts of the Old Testament. However, in regard to the question of physical death, it really makes no major difference whether one assumes a solar day or a longer period, because God's admonition acted as a direct warning that the penalty would be physical death.

Where in the Old Testament does any writer ever speak of spiritual death? Each time the Hebrew word for "death" ("muwth") is used in the Old Testament (791 times), it always deals with physical death. [For a definition of each variation of the word "death" in the Old Testament, see: Francis Brown, et al, *The New Brown-Driver-Briggs-Gesenius Hebrew and English Lexicon* (Peabody, MA: Hendrickson Publishers, 1979), pp. 559a-560]

This reign of death which prevails over all that is born cannot be the normal state of a world created by God. Nature suffers from a curse which it cannot have brought upon itself, as it is not morally free.

Dr. F. Godet

The process of physical dying began the moment Adam bit the forbidden fruit. Adam's physical death became an immediate certainty. In a real sense, Adam did die at that time; it simply took a while to realize its completion. Commentaries verify that the Hebrew idiom used by God to warn Adam clearly communicates the certainty that physical death would result from disobedience. The physical death of every human and animal — living or yet to be born — became an absolute certainty at the moment of Adam's rebellion. The possibility of physical immortality on this planet was gone.

Adam's disobedience also resulted in spiritual separation from God, as Ross proposes. Adam immediately realized his own guilt, nakedness and impurity before a holy God. Adam's spiritual separation from his Creator was symbolized by his lifetime expulsion from the Garden. No longer could he walk and talk face-to-face with his Creator.

Creation and Time continues by claiming, "*I Corinthians 15:21 also must refer to spiritual death rather than to physical death.*" [p. 61]

The fact that Paul is referring to physical death (not just spiritual, as Ross contends) is obvious in the context. Paul is writing of people who have *physically* died. He is writing of Christ's *physical* death and *physical* resurrection. Paul's reference to physical death resulting from Adam could hardly be stated more clearly! I Corinthians 15, Genesis 2-3, and Romans 5:12f all testify to the fact that physical death was involved. As theologian Gleason Archer observes, *"The universality of this guilt is attested by its observed effect - the death penalty. Physical death came upon all men from Adam's time onward. This shows that the moral law was binding upon mankind before the Mosaic law was ever revealed."* [Gleason L. Archer Jr., *The Epistle to the Romans* (Grand Rapids, MI: Baker Book House, 1959), p. 31]

This entire chapter, written by Paul, emphasizes the futility of hope in Christ if He did not physically raise from the dead. The Greeks had no problem believing in a spiritual resurrection, but they could not comprehend a physical one. To them, all physical material was evil, only the spiritual was pure. Paul combats this Greek philosophy by showing that through Adam, the body had been contaminated and made subject to death. Christ, the Son of God, defeated physical death and rose in bodily form. If Dr. Ross desires to treat this vital chapter as if it is referring to spiritual death and resurrection, he is fighting against the clear teaching of Paul.

Creation and Time claims "<u>the</u> penalty for sin is spiritual death... Thus the atonement had to be made by a spiritual Being (meaning Jesus Christ)" [p. 64 — emphasis added]

The Bible tells us, *"For the wages of sin is death."* (Romans 6:23) This verse does not classify death as merely "spiritual." Most commentaries acknowledge that spiritual death is <u>a</u> penalty for sin. It is clear, however, from the context of Romans 6:23 that physical death is also indicated.

Hebrews chapter 2 also reveals the true connection between sin and death. Here the humanity of Christ is emphasized. *"For both He who sanctifies and those who are sanctified are all from one Father* [humanity]; *for which reason He is not ashamed to call them brethren"* (Hebrews 2:11, *NASB*). We are told from this passage that Christ *"tasted death"* (verse 9, literally translated: "fully experienced or partook of death") so that *"through death He might render powerless him who had the power of death, that is, the devil"* (Hebrews 2:14, *NASB*). This chapter clearly refers to <u>physical</u> humanity experiencing <u>physical</u> death. Moreover, it explicitly attributes the power of death to the devil. Could the author of Hebrews have made it any more clear that physical death is a penalty for sin? Certainly not! Dr. Ross ignores the clear and universal voice of Scripture when he insists that only spiritual death is a result of sin.

Note: In this quote, Creation and Time refers to Christ as a "spiritual Being." This is interesting since this is essentially the same term Ross uses to distinguish humans (spirit beings) from the hominids (spiritless animals that looked like humans) and other "non-spirit beings such as bower birds, elephants, and chimpanzees." [pp. 140-141]

Dr. Ross claims that millions of years ago God began progressively creating more human-like apes (hominids). He says, "Starting about 2 to 4 million years [or at least 1 million years] ago God began creating man-like mammals." ["Genesis One, Dinosaurs and Cavemen," audiotape (Pasadena, CA: Reasons to Believe, 1989)] Although some of these creatures looked completely human (e.g., Cro-Magnon, Neanderthal), "used tools... buried their dead and painted on cave walls," they were actually animals and "had no spirits," according to Dr. Ross. ["Genesis One, Dinosaurs and Cavemen"] "The hominid species may have gone extinct before, or as a result of, the appearance of modern man." [Creation and Time, p. 88, etc.; Fingerprint of God, p. 160, also see pp. 159-160]

How many Christians can hear such a description and not feel uncomfortable? Is this really the way God would do things? The implication that Neanderthal and Cro-Magnon had no spirits seems absurd. Even most secular scientists agree these were people — and 100% human. Both are classified as Homo sapiens.

CLAIM: Creation was subjected to futility from its very beginning.

Romans 8:20 states, "For the creation was subjected to futility, not willingly, but because of Him who subjected it in hope." Creation and Time teaches that creation was subjected to futility from its very beginning. Therefore *"the process of decay has been in effect since the universe was created."* [p. 67]

FALSE. God created a paradise. Numerous biblical theologians heartily disagree with Ross on this point.

Bible commentators speak in an almost unanimous voice that the futility referred to in this verse is a result of sin. Linski states, *"The creation was subjected to man before the fall but not subject 'to vainness.'—This noun (futility in the NIV) is derived from 'mataios', 'vain' in the sense of failure to reach the proper end, to accomplish the intended purpose."* [R.C.H. Linski, *The Interpretation of St. Paul's Epistle to the Romans* (Columbus, Ohio: Wartsburg Press, 1945), p. 533]

Godet states, *"This reign of death which prevails over all that is born cannot be the normal state of a world created by God. Nature suffers from a curse which it cannot have brought upon itself, as it is not morally free."* [F. Godet, *Commentary on St. Paul's Epistle to the Romans* (NYC: Funk & Wagnells Publishers, 1883), p. 314]

Everett Harrison teaches, *"Instead of considering the future simply from the standpoint of the redeemed, Paul enlarges the perspective to include the whole creation... because the creation's own deliverance from the frustration imposed on it by the fall cannot come until that time... The groaning of the creation looks back to its subjection to frustration, whereas the pangs of childbirth anticipate the age of renewal. In other words, the same sufferings are at once a result and a prophecy."* [Everett F. Harrison, edited by Frank E. Gabelein, *Expositors Bible Commentary*, Vol. 10 (Grand Rapids, MI: Zondervan, 1976), p. 94]

If Dr. Ross insists that these verses teach that God created a world in "vain," a world that was created for frustration, then he stands dangerously alone in the world of biblical theology. It is obvious that his belief must only be based on current scientific "facts" for it cannot be supported from biblical exegesis.

CLAIM: "Church father" Origen and Isaiah supported pre-Fall "bondage to decay"

Dr. Ross: *"Those who interpret Romans 8 as I do are said to place science above the Bible and to stretch the text beyond reasonable limits to accommodate science. But can such a charge apply to third-century church leader Origen? ...He says it (Romans 8) implies that decay has been in effect in the natural world since the creation of the universe... it seems unreasonable to accuse him of submitting to the pressure of the scientific community."* [p. 67]

MISLEADING. Origen's belief is insignificant to the argument. Although Origen is considered to be a Church Father due to the survival of his prolific writings; he was extremely controversial. There are numerous problems in his theology. Many of his beliefs were far from the mainstream of more respected Church Fathers. (See section on Church Fathers for further information on the beliefs of Origen)

It is important to note that Origen's view of Romans 8 was based on the Greek philosophy of his day; it was not biblical. *Creation and Time* fails to consider the context of Origen's statement. Because of Origen's commitment to the Greek philosophy which taught that all material things were necessarily evil and corrupt, *"wherever bodies are, corruption immediately follows."* [Origen, *Ante-Nicene Fathers*, Vol. 4, p. 345, also see pp. 264, 341-342] He could not conceive of a material world created in perfection and harmony. Origen claimed that just as there will be a new creation after this present world is destroyed, there was also a world previous to this present world. He claimed that this previous world consisted of spiritual beings which were punished because of their "excessive mental defects." Their punishment consisted of being given physical bodies in this "material" world.

We see, therefore, that Origen's views were perfectly consistent with the Greek philosophy of his time that taught the spirit is pure and good but anything physical is evil. Therefore, both Origen and Dr. Ross can be said to have adopted erroneous interpretations of Romans 8 because of their uncritical acceptance of the teachings common to their times.

In proposing that Romans 8:19f teaches that creation has always been subject to decay and futility, *Creation and Time* further suggests that *"the text might refer, as well, to another kind of decay: the disorder in people's life and underline{environment} that resulted from rebellion against God. ...Isaiah 24:5 describes underline{the devastation of the planet that results from the insubordination of human beings to God."* [p. 67 — emphasis added] In other words, Dr. Ross suggests that Paul and Isaiah were referring to human-caused environmental pollution, thousands of years before environmentalism was in vogue.

FALSE. This is another example of poor exegesis. Whatever Paul and Isaiah's position on environmentalism, these verses don't prove Ross's claim. These verses do not refer to any devastation caused by man's irresponsibility, but to the _future_ judgment of the earth by God. Isaiah prophesies God's destruction of the earth. At first glance, when reading the *NASB* translation, these verses may *seem* to teach what Ross proposes: *"The earth is also polluted by its inhabitants, for they transgressed laws, violated statutes, broke the everlasting covenant"* (*NASB*).

1. The *NIV* and *NKJV* use the word "defiled" rather than "polluted." Man is the defilement, having broken God's laws and covenant.

2. Isaiah 24-27 is known as Isaiah's apocalypse. A closer examination of this section reveals that verse 24:5 is not talking about man's past or current failures, but about a *future* defilement and about a future judgment of God upon the earth. It is widely agreed that this section deals with the Tribulation period and the beginning of the Millennial age.

3. The devastation of earth's environment is done by God, not by man. Isaiah describes what will happen, *"Behold, the LORD lays the earth waste, devastates it, distorts its surface ... The earth will be completely laid waste and completely despoiled, for the LORD has spoken this word. The earth mourns and withers, the world fades and withers ... Therefore, a curse devours the earth...."* (Isaiah 24:1,3-4,6, *NASB*) The context of these verses certainly demonstrates that God is the one who ultimately destroys the earth's environment in a future act of judgment, not mankind!

Dr. Ross has supported a doubtful interpretation of Romans 8:19f with an erroneous interpretation of Isaiah 24:5.

Biblical Considerations

CLAIM: The Flood was local, not global.

Dr. Ross teaches that the Flood did not cover the entire earth nor all the mountains of the day. Rather, he claims that Noah and animals floated on a shallow, temporary inland sea (22 feet deep) somehow covering the Mesopotamian region. Ross says earth's entire human population was limited to this area. His publications teach that most of the animals of the world were not affected, only those animals in Mesopotamia. (Of course, few, if any, of these animals would have been unique to the region.)

According to Dr. Ross, all of today's land animals and birds are *not* descended from the creatures on the Ark. [*Creation and Time*, p. 73; Hugh Ross, *Facts & Faith*, Reasons to Believe's quarterly newsletter, multiple part article on the Flood (1989-91), especially parts 7 and 8 (Fall and Winter 1990); Hugh Ross, "Noah's Floating Zoo," *Facts & Faith*, Vol. 4 (Fall 1990), pp. 4-5; Hugh Ross, "The Flood," audiotape (Pasadena, CA: Reasons to Believe, 1990)]

FALSE. The Bible is abundantly clear that the Flood was global and that every land animal and bird on the face of the earth was wiped out (Genesis 6:7, 7:21-23), except those on the Ark.

We do not know of any serious Hebrew scholar that would respect Ross's strange interpretation. Dr. Gleason Archer (to whom Ross often looks for support) conclusively demonstrates that the Bible describes a universal, global flood. [Gleason L. Archer, Jr., *A Survey of Old Testament Introduction* (Chicago: Moody Press, 1979), pp. 202-211] Even secular scholars know that the Bible definitely describes a global Flood. The Genesis account could hardly be more clear.

Ross rejects a global Flood with massive geologic effects because it conflicts with his belief in a billions-of-years old earth with sediments and fossils laid down over millions and billions of years.

Following Ross's rather bizarre scenario, after thousands of years every human being still remained in the relatively small Mesopotamian region. Then, for no apparent reason, God required Noah to consume 120 years of his life building a huge boat to save representative animals which really didn't need to be saved. Most, if not all, of these animals were alive and well in other parts of the world. Dry land was just over the horizon all along. Despite the lack of necessity, God kept Noah trapped in this boat full of animals under these strange circumstances for over a year!

For several reasons, it is important for Ross to deny that Noah's flood was global. First, the majority of secular scientists deny that the biblical flood could have occurred. Thus, Dr. Ross remains consistent in his support of modern science, even if the biblical record seems to be contradicted. Second, the global effect of the Flood is a foundational tenet that supports a young-earth position. If Dr. Ross were to concede that the Flood was global, as described in the Bible, then he would lose many of the scientific "facts" he now uses as proofs for an ancient earth.

The Bible says the Flood was global, not local

1. ALL MOUNTAINS COVERED. The waters *"rose greatly on the earth, and all the high mountains under the entire heavens were covered. The waters rose and covered the mountains to a depth of more than twenty feet"* (Genesis 7:19-20, *NIV*). Furthermore, the waters remained at this awesome, mountain-covering depth for 5 months! (See Genesis 7:18-24, 8:1-5) In one of his audiotapes, Dr. Ross made the incredible claim that *"the word 'high' is not in the original. It's not there. ...it's not in the Hebrew."* [Hugh Ross, "The Flood," Part 1, audiotape (Pasadena, CA: Reasons to Believe, 1990)] Dr. Ross is completely wrong on this point. The Hebrew word for "high" (Hebrew:

"gaboah") is most assuredly in the oldest Hebrew manu-scripts as well as in modern Hebrew Bibles.

2. ALL AIR-BREATHING LAND-ANIMALS KILLED. The world's entire population of air-breathing land animals died in the Flood, except for those preserved on the Ark. Genesis 6:17 — *"I am going to bring floodwaters on the earth to destroy <u>all</u> life under the heavens, <u>every</u> creature that has the breath of life in it. Everything on earth will perish."* Genesis 7:4 — *"...I will wipe from the face of the earth <u>every</u> living creature I have made"* (NIV). Genesis 7:21-23 — *"<u>Every</u> living thing that moved on the earth perished ...<u>all</u> the creatures... <u>Every-thing</u> on dry land that had the breath of life in its nostrils died. <u>Every living thing on the face of the earth</u> was wiped out; men and animals and the creatures that move along the ground and the birds of the air were wiped from the earth. Only Noah was left, and those with him in the ark"* (NIV). Genesis 8:21 — *"...never again will I destroy <u>all</u> living creatures, as I have done"* (NIV). Genesis 9:11 — *"...Never again will <u>all</u> life be cut off by the waters of a flood; never again will there be a flood to destroy <u>the earth</u>"* (NIV).

3. ALL LAND-DWELLING AIR-BREATHING ANIMALS ARE DESCENDED FROM THOSE SAVED ON THE ARK. Genesis 7:2-4 — *"Take with you seven of every kind of clean animal, a male and its mate, and two of every kind of unclean animal, a male and its mate, and also seven of every kind of bird, male and female, <u>to keep their various kinds alive throughout the earth</u> ...I will wipe from the face of the earth every living creature I have made"* (NIV). Genesis 7:15 — *"Pairs of all creatures that have the breath of life in them came to Noah and entered the ark"* (NIV). Genesis 7:23 — *"Every living thing on the face of the earth was wiped out; men and animals and the creatures that move along the ground and the birds of the air were wiped from the earth. Only Noah was left, and those with him in the ark"* (NIV). If only those animals in a specific geographic region died, it would have been unnecessary to protect pairs in the Ark for the express purpose of preventing their extinction. Surely there would be representatives of their kinds in other areas. If, on the other hand, there had been some unique kinds in the path of a local flood, then it would

seem more logical to send representative pairs out of the area, rather than to the Ark, as God did. Certainly the birds could have flown to the safety of dry land. If the Flood had been local, God could also have simply sent Noah and family out of the area.

4. THE ARK WAS HUGE. Until the first metal ships were constructed in modern times, the Ark was the largest ship ever built. If the Flood were local, the Ark was unnecessarily large — big enough to house representative pairs of every created kind of air-breathing land animal on earth.

5. A "CATACLYSM," NOT A MERE FLOOD. Both Hebrew (Old Testament) and Greek (New Testament) use words to describe Noah's flood which are different than the ordinary words for "flood." In this way, Noah's flood was represented as a totally unique occurrence. [Hebrew: "Mabbool" / Greek: "Kataklusmos" (cataclysm)]

The message of the Bible is clear for those who will read it and seek to find out its meaning. The problem comes when people bring their preconceived notions to the Bible and attempt to make the Word fit their ideas. This is not the fault of the Bible, but of the persons who force the Bible to say what they want it to say.

Josh McDowell

---

6. GOD'S RAINBOW PROMISE. God promised never again to send a global flood (Genesis 8:21, 8:8-17). The rainbow sign was a promise to all living creatures. Genesis 9:9-17: *"I now establish my covenant with you... and with every living creature that was with you--the birds, the livestock and all the wild animals, all those that came out of the ark with you — every living creature on earth. ...Never again will all life be cut off by the waters of a flood; never again will there be a flood to destroy the earth. ...This is the sign of the covenant I am making between me and you and every living creature with you... I have set my*

rainbow in the clouds, and it will be the sign of the covenant between me <u>and the earth</u>. ...Whenever ...the rainbow appears in the clouds, I will remember my covenant between me and you <u>and all living creatures of every kind</u>. Never again will the waters become a flood to destroy <u>all life</u>. ...remember the everlasting covenant between God and <u>all living creatures of every kind on the earth</u>. ...between me and <u>all life on the earth</u>" (NIV). If this promise was not made to all creatures on earth, then God has broken His promise. Local floods have repeatedly killed hundreds and even thousands of animals since Noah's time.

7. WHY STAY IN THE ARK FOR A YEAR?! Noah was in the Ark for more than a year, not just 40 days. 53 weeks is absurdly long to stay in a boat for a local flood, but it makes perfect sense if the Flood was global.

8. THE DOVE. After the water had been going down for 4 months, the dove could still find no suitable ground (Genesis 8:9). This does not describe a local flood.

9. THE WHOLE EARTH WAS DEVASTATED. God said, *"I am surely going to destroy both them* [the people] *and the earth"* (Genesis 6:13b, NIV). The global extent of the Flood is referred to more than 30 times in Genesis 6-9 alone! Isaiah 54:9 states, *"...I swore that the waters of Noah would never again cover the earth"* (NIV). Peter delivered a clear global warning, confirming that God created the earth, devastated it by the Flood, and will one day destroy it again by fire (II Peter 3:5-7). Peter certainly did not mean that just a local area on earth would be burned. Just as the Flood was global, so will be the final judgment. How could the Bible be any more clear concerning the global nature of the Flood?! Or, if this was actually a local flood, how could the Bible have been any more misleading about its extent?!

CLAIM: The Creation account is told from the perspective of an observer on earth.

Creation and Time proposes that the Creation account should be understood as if you were seeing it take place from upon the surface of the earth. Dr. Ross feels that this perspective is provided in Genesis 1:2, *"and the Spirit of God was hovering over the waters."* He states that you must understand this perspective from which Creation is observed in order to avoid *"the seeming futility of the attempt to integrate Genesis with the scientific record... the view looking upward and around from this vantage point (upon the face of the ocean) makes a huge difference in understanding the sequence of creation events. From misplacing the perspective in the heavens, it appears that light was created after the earth."* [p. 149]

Dr. Ross claims that Genesis 1 describes Creation from the point of view of one standing on the earth; and that the sun, moon and stars did not become *visible* until the fourth day. [*Creation and Time*, p. 149; *The Fingerprint of God*, pp. 165-169; "Why Big Bang Opponents Never Say Die"]

> FALSE. There is nothing within the biblical record that suggests Genesis 1:2 intends to direct the reader to some proper viewing reference. And even if an earth-bound perspective was correct, the facts are not changed.
>
> *Creation and Time* does not support this earth-bound perspective conclusion with any language studies, syntax, context or cultural significance. Rather than reevaluating the "scientific facts," *Creation and Time* suggests that we reinterpret the Bible's Creation account. Is this suggestion for establishing a new perspective legitimate? Does Ross point to any hermeneutic evidence for this "vital" interpretation? No.
>
> More importantly, even if Ross were correct about the possibility of an earth-bound perspective for this passage, there is still a problem. Changing perspective does not change a clear, propositional teaching. Genesis 1 explicitly states the order of creative events. Ross's earth-bound perspective does not somehow give him a license to reinterpret these clear statements of Scripture without sound hermeneutic support.

CLAIM: Most stars and planets were created before the first day.

Creation and Time teaches that the sun, moon and stars were not created on the fourth "day" of Creation. Dr. Ross claims that most stars existed long before earth's creation. In fact, he suggests that God's creation of the heavens and the earth was not limited to the six days of Creation recorded in the Bible, it began long before the Creation Week began. He says, *"The creation of the universe that took place prior to the first creative day."* [p. 52 — emphasis added] This is again confirmed in his previous book where he claims, *"According to Genesis 1, the origin of the universe predates the six days of creation."* [*The Fingerprint of God* (p. 159)]

Ross teaches that prior to the Creation week approximately 10-15 billion years of stellar evolution occurred. He believes the stars were not created instantaneously; rather, they evolved by the physical laws of nature put into place by God. [*Creation and Time*, p. 52; *The Fingerprint of God*, pp. 158-159, 165-169]

"This entire process of stellar evolution is by natural process alone. We do not have to invoke Divine intervention at any stage in the history of the life-cycle of the stars that we observe." [Hugh Ross, "Species Development: Natural Process or Divine Action," audiotape (Pasadena, CA: Reasons to Believe, 1990)]

In fact, according to *Creation and Time*, many stars had long ceased to exist by the time of Adam's creation. *"The planets and life-essential elements are the burned-up remains – i.e., ashes – of* [the Big Bang's] *hydrogen gas."* [p. 131 — emphasis added]

Furthermore, he speculates that even the first life forms were created prior to the Creation Week: *"Scientific evidence for ocean life predating land life poses no threat either. The Spirit of God 'brooded' over the face of the waters (Genesis 1:2), possibly creating life in the oceans before the events of the six creation days begin."* [p. 153]

FALSE. Scripture is clear. The sun, moon and stars were created on the fourth day, not the first or before (Genesis 1:14-19). Hebrew scholars such as E.J. Young confirm this. [E.J. Young, *Studies in Genesis One* (Presbyterian and Reformed Publishing Co., 1964), p. 95]

Further, Ross's claim that the creation of the stars or any-thing else in the universe came before the first day is a plain contradiction of Exodus 20:11. Here God wrote with His own finger and reemphasized the truth that only He could know: *"For in six days the Lord made the heavens and the earth, the sea and all that is in them..."* (NASB). This verse does not say that the six day week is a commemorative representation of a Creation epoch. No, God set in stone the fact that He created everything that exists in six days, and rested on the seventh. There is no biblical way to place star and sun formation before the fourth day. [*See:* James Stambaugh, "Star Formation and Genesis 1," "Impact" article 251, *Acts and Facts*, Vol. 23, No. 5 (El Cajon, CA: Institute for Creation Research, May 1994)]

If all of Dr. Ross's interpretations of Genesis 1 were true, then for thousands of years the vast majority of Jews and Christians grossly misunderstood Genesis. They thought that all Creation took place during this week in the plain order stated and that the Creation Week consisted of real, non-overlapping days which began five, literal days before the creation of Adam. If Ross is correct, then it was not until very recently that Progressive Creationists, thanks to the aid of modern science, finally discovered the correct interpretation. Does this really seem likely?

God surely intended the basic meaning of Genesis to be un-derstood, even by relatively ignorant and fallen men. After all, these are the beginning, foundational chapters of the Bible, filled with information that all humanity was meant to know and understand.

The Bible teaches that animals were created for man. Adam and his children were to rule over the animal kingdom. If Pro-gressive Creationists are correct, Adam was not created until the vast majority of earth's animal population had already died. Remember those millions of fossils that would have been under Adam's feet in the Progressive Creation scenario? In fact, by the time Adam arrived, many diverse kinds would al-ready have become extinct! Most people can see that the Crea-tion story makes a lot more sense the way the Church has his-torically understood it.

CLAIM: The simplest, most natural reading of Genesis 1 is that the days were long ages.

Dr. Ross argues against the historic belief of the Church that the simplest, most natural reading of Genesis chapter 1 is that of literal days. He assures readers that this was not his experience. Ross says that his first reading of the Creation account convinced him that the Bible supported "days" that were long periods of time and were totally consistent with the findings of modern science. [pp. 143-147]

Ross: *"I was a young man of* seventeen. *I came at the Bible fresh, without input, and I tackled it on my own and, you know, immediately rejected the view that they were six, consecutive twenty-four hour days. I knew right away those days were not twenty-four hours."* [Hugh Ross, "Creation Days," audio-tape (1990)]

FALSE. For thousands of years, Jews and Christians have read the Bible and easily seen that God's Word describes a thousands-of-years-old earth created in six literal days with the sun, moon and stars created on the fourth day.

It is apparent that Dr. Ross does not speak for all Progressive Creationists when he asserts that the simplest reading of Genesis 1 leads to a belief in long creative ages. Gleason Archer says, *"From a superficial reading of Genesis 1, the impression received is that the entire creative process took place in six twenty-four-hour days."* [Gleason L. Archer, Jr., *A Survey of Old Testament Introduction* (Chicago: Moody Press, 1979), p. 181] Leading Progressive Creationist Pattle P. T. Pun has written, *"It is apparent that the most straightforward understanding of the Genesis record, without regard to all of the hermeneutical considerations suggested by science, is that God created heaven and earth in six solar days, that man was created in the sixth day, that death and chaos entered the world after the Fall of Adam and Eve, that all of the fossils were the result of the catastrophic universal deluge which spared only Noah's family and the animals therewith."* [Pattle P.T. Pun, "A Theology of Progressive Creationism," *Journal of the American Scientific Affiliation,* Vol. 39, No. 1 (Ipswich, MA: March 1987), p. 14 — emphasis added]

As a 17 year old, Ross first read this Scripture with the goal of comparing the Creation account to his knowledge of "scientific facts." He was already convinced of the Big Bang and the age of the universe. He was already convinced of the progression of life-forms found in the "geologic column." Is it any wonder that as a teenager with an uncritical acceptance of science, he would find the "simplest" reading of the Bible to agree with his preconceived views?

---

*All scientists (young-earth or old-earth) have
the same evidences from nature.
Their interpretation of that data is
often dependent upon
foundational assumptions and presuppositions.*

His reading of the Bible was also done without knowledge of Hebrew or the rules of proper hermeneutics, and without any real understanding of biblical theology. Yet, the conclusions he arrived at by his "simple" reading are what he still teaches today. His further Bible study and training have not affected his original opinion. Consider Ross's own words about his first reading of the Flood account:

"I kind of read through the text and it <u>seemed obvious to me</u> that <u>it had to be a local flood</u>, not a global flood, and <u>I was shocked</u> to discover that there are all these Christians, and even Christian scholars that held to a global flood. And I wanted to figure out, you know, how did this happen? You know, <u>how did people get off track like this</u>? And <u>maybe I'm speaking a little bit pridefully here</u>, but, you know, that's how I was operating in my youth, you know. Where did they get off on this?" [Hugh Ross, *The Flood*, Part II, audio-tape (Reasons to Believe, 1990)]

It is apparent that Dr. Ross's teachings concerning the length of the Creation Week and small extent of the Flood had little to do with real study of the Hebrew syntax or literary genre. He came to his conclusions based upon his assumptions about scientific "fact." His arguments do not change the Bible's statements. The simplest reading of the Bible supports a global flood and six 24 hour Creation days. This is well-known among theologians, both liberal and conservative. This has been the "simple" teaching of the church since its inception.

Note: It is also important to realize that, according to Dr. Ross: *"Each of God's creation days is several hundred million years long."* [Hugh Ross, *Genesis 1: A Scientific Perspective*, Revised Edition (Sierra Madre, CA: Wiseman Productions, 1983), p. 11]

Ross also says the earth was created about 4.6 billion years ago, and that some (or all) of the Creation days partially overlapped. He teaches that we are currently still in the seventh day — a day that will not end until the beginning of the New Heavens and New Earth. [*Creation and Time*, pp. 59, 91-118; *Fingerprint of God* , pp. 146-155]

We must ask ourselves — can all this information really be gathered by a <u>simple</u> reading of Scripture? The obvious answer is no.

CLAIM: The Bible says the earth is very old.

Ross: *"The brief span of a 3000-year terrestrial history (in context of the wisdom literature) seems an inadequate metaphor for God's eternality. The fact that the Bible does consider the antiquity of the founding of the earth a suitable metaphor for God's eternality suggests the biblical view of a very ancient earth."* [p.52] Ross also claims that, *"Habakkuk 3:6 directly declares that the mountains are 'ancient' and the hills are 'age-old.' In 2 Peter 3:5, the heavens (the stars and the universe) are said to have existed 'long ago.'"* [p. 52]

MISLEADING. A thousands-of-years-old history is significant and ancient in the context of short-lived humans. The verses referenced by Dr. Ross provide no indication of billions of years. To the contrary, the Bible indicates that the cosmos is thousands of years old.

The billionaire that increases his fiscal year profits by a mere $3,000 is less than enthusiastic. Yet, a poverty stricken person who receives an additional $3,000 (perhaps doubling his income) views the same amount as very significant. The point is this: perhaps Dr. Ross has become so accustomed to talking about billions-of-years that 3,000 or 6,000 sounds like an insignificant drop in a bucket. However, when talking about earth history, three millennia is a very large period of time indeed. From a human perspective, we come and go — only the mountains and God continue on after our lifetimes.

Think back approximately 3,000 years ago. David was the second King of the young nation of Israel. The birth of Christ was still a millennium in the future. The United States would not become a nation for another 2.7 millennia. Certainly, when compared to the finite lives of mortal men, three millennia provides a meaningful statement about God's eternality.

Psalm 90:1-5 is one of the passages referred to by Ross. Here, the author Moses uses figures of speech to illustrate God's timelessness. He compares short periods of time to long periods of time — a day or a watch in the night (4 hours) compared to a millennium or the age of mountains. Moses was justified in considering a millennium to be a great length of time. He used this figure of speech to emphasize God's timelessness.

In another passage referenced by Ross, the apostle Peter states that the stars and the universe began "of old" or "long ago" (II Peter 3:5, Greek: "ekpalai"). Peter previously used that same word to indicate that God's judgment is awaiting false teachers. *"In their greed these teachers will exploit you with stories they have made up. Their condemnation has* long *[same word: ekpalai] been hanging over them..."* (II Peter 2:3, *NIV*). Clearly, the word does not require or imply a billions-of-years meaning, and therefore Dr. Ross has no Scriptural reason to assume that II Peter 3:5 refers to billions of years.

The other verses referenced by Hugh Ross contain one of four Hebrew words: *'az, 'olam, 'eythan,* or *'ad.* A simple check in any good Hebrew lexicon or concordance indicates that none of these words are capable of demonstrating that the earth and universe must be billions, millions or even thousands of years old. All four of the words are used in reference to events in the near or distant past, and none provide any indication of the date of Creation. [Francis Brown, et al, *The New Brown-Driver-Briggs-Gesenius Hebrew and English Lexicon* (Peabody, MA: Hendrickson Publishers, 1979), 'az: p. 23a; 'eythan: p. 450b; 'ad: p. 723b; 'olam: p. 761b]

CLAIM: God's days are not our days Psalm 90:4 and 2 Peter 3:8.

Creation and Time quotes from Psalm 90:4 in an attempt to show that for God the meaning of "days" is not the same as man's: *"The same author of Genesis (Moses) wrote in Psalm 90:4, 'For a thousand years in your sight are like a day that has just gone by, or like a watch [4 hours] in the night.' Moses seems to state that just as God's ways are not our ways (Isaiah 55:9), God's days are not our days."* [p. 45] Ross proceeds to use this as Scriptural evidence that the days of Creation are not literal days.

FALSE. Dr. Ross has connected two topics which do not have a legitimate relationship. Psalm 90:4 and II Peter 3:8 are not relevant to the discussion of literal Creation days.

It is clear that the intended meaning of the authors (Moses and Peter) had nothing to do with the measurement of time, but with God's nature. II Peter 3:8 says, *"With the Lord a day is like a thousand years, and a thousand years are like a day"* (NIV). The point made by both Moses and Peter is that God is beyond time limitations; He is timeless! Peter is not claiming that there is some special time zone called "God Standard Time" where one God-day equals 1,000 human-years. If this were true, then it would also be fair to say that 1,000 God-years are equal to one human-day (i.e., 1 God-day = 1,000 human-years = 1,000 God-years = 1 human-day). The result is absurd and meaningless. Peter and Moses are simply using figurative language to make the point that God is not limited by time. Since God's nature, and not time, is emphasized in these verses, they add nothing to our discussion about the age of the earth.

Importantly, the "days" in Genesis 1 are modified by physical, human measurements of time such as "evening," "morning" and consecutive sequencing. This is one of the strong evidences that these describe 24-hour type days.

CLAIM: The use of "morning and evening" in Genesis 1 does not indicate literal days. The Hebrew word for "morning" in Genesis 1 is metaphorical.

In response to Genesis's use of "evening and morning" in the description of each of the six Creation days, *Creation and Time* argues against the literal understanding of these terms. It claims that the Hebrew word for morning, "boqer" should be understood metaphorically, not literally. To substantiate this metaphorical usage, it claims that boqer "also means 'sunrise,' 'coming of light,' 'beginning of day,' 'break of day,' or 'dawning', with possible metaphoric usage." [p. 46] Ross argues that "morning" and the Creation days should therefore be understood metaphorically, not literally.

FALSE. This is yet another incorrect claim.

Boqer is used 205 times in the Old Testament. None of these uses are obviously metaphoric. Further, both of the references given by Ross to document this point prove to be in error.

Brown-Driver-Briggs-Gesenius Hebrew-English Lexicon makes no mention of boqer used as metaphor. This is also true for Ross's other resource, *The Theological Wordbook of the Old Testament* by Harris, Archer & Waltke, which states in part, *"boqer may denote "early" or "promptly" as in 'God will help her right early' (lit. 'at the turning of morning'...), but the case can not be proved."* [Vol. 1, p. 125 — emphasis added]. It seems that the normal way to understand boqer is the normal, literal meaning of morning. Any other translation (i.e., metaphoric) remains unproved.

The use of "evening and morning" are an excellent evidence that the Creation week consisted of literal days. Since we have shown that the normal, literal interpretation of the words "morning" and "evening" is preferred, Ross's argument is inappropriate.

It is also important to note that the words "morning and evening" are combined with the word "day" (yom) 38 times *outside* of Genesis 1 — always with literal 24-hour day meaning. There is no reason to think that the Creation narrative uses a meaning different than all the other Scriptural references.

CLAIM: Because the word "day" in Genesis 2:4 refs to the entire Creation week, there is more reason to believe the first six days were not literal.

Ross: *"In Genesis 2:4 the word for "day," yôm, refers to the entire creation week, demonstrating its flexible usage."* [Hugh Ross, "The Creation-Date Controversy," *The Real Issue* (Dallas, TX: Christian Leadership Ministries, 1994)] *"Here the word day refers to all six creation days (and the creation of the universe that took place prior to the first creative day). Obviously, then, this is a period longer than twenty-four hours."* [p. 52]

MISLEADING: We do not know of any young-earth creationist that would argue against the fact that the Hebrew word for "day" (yom) can refer to a period of time longer than 24 hours. Genesis 2:4 is certainly one of these instances, as the context of the verse clearly indicates. This is not, however, an evidence for an old earth.

The days of the Creation week give every indication that they are normal length days. They are each modified by an ordinal number (1st, 2nd, 3rd, etc.) and by the terms "morning and evening." God stated in the strongest of terms that Creation took place during six normal days.

CLAIM: The "uniqueness" of the seventh day indicates the days of Creation were not normal days.

Dr. Ross: *"The seventh day continues through Old and New Testament times and on into the future."* [Hugh Ross, "The Creation-Date Controversy," *The Real Issue* (Dallas, TX: Christian Leadership Ministries, 1994)] *"It seems reasonable to conclude then, given the parallelism of the Genesis creation accounts, that the first six days may also have been long time periods."* [pp. 48-49]

FALSE. The seventh day was a 24-hour type day, as were the first six days.

1. UNFAIR REASONING. Dr. Ross points out that there is no "morning and evening" recorded for the seventh day. Ironically, because these three words were not included, he claims that the seventh day is a long period of time. We can only conclude that he makes this argument with tongue-in-cheek, for Progressive Creationists claim the phrase "evening and morning" is metaphoric. Dr. Ross would argue for long ages even if Day Seven did include this phrase, just as he does with the other days.

2. DAY SEVEN IS COMPLETED. The Wording of Genesis 2:2-3 shows that the 7th day of rest is completed.

    Note what the verse in question actually says: *"And by the seventh day God completed His work which He had done; and He rested on the seventh day from all His work which He had done. Then God blessed the seventh day and sanctified it, because in it He rested from all His work which God had created and made"* (Genesis 2:2-3).

    Although there is no mention of "evening and morning", the meaning seems clear.

    RESTED. The word "rested" in verse 3 ("Qal," perfect, third masculine singular) indicates completed action, God rested (past tense).

    BLESSED. God "blessed" the seventh day. Blessings are the opposite of curses. It is difficult to understand how God's curse could occur during a time that was specially blessed by God. The concepts cannot go together for they are totally opposite. How can one understand the concept of blessing for this "continued long age" when Romans states the following? *"For the anxious longing of the creation waits eagerly for the revealing of the sons of God. For the creation was subjected to futility, not of its own will, but because of Him who subjected it in the hope that the creation itself also will be set free from its slavery to corruption into the freedom of the glory of the children of God. For we know that the whole creation groans and suffers the pains of childbirth together until now"* (Romans 8:19-22).

SANCTIFIED. God sanctified the seventh day. Sanctified ("piel," imperfect, third masculine singular) refers to *setting something apart* as consecrated, holy and sacred. It is an act of dedication. In this way, the seventh day was set apart from all other days. The seventh day was sanctified, unlike the days that had preceded it or that would come after it. It is unlikely that the Fall of man and God's cursing of nature occurred on that special, holy and sacred day. Jews and the Church have historically understood that these sad events came sometime *after* the end of that day.

GOD'S TESTIMONY. God's himself indicates that the seventh day is completed — and that the 24-hour Sabbath was patterned after Day Seven — when He asserts, *"...in six days the Lord made the heavens and the earth, the sea, and all that is in them, and rested the seventh day... Therefore the Lord blessed the Sabbath day and hallowed it"* (Exodus 20:11, *NKJV*). This passage is written in perfect tense, indicating completed actions. The seventh Creation day was, in effect, the first Sabbath. In context, there is no reason to assume these are figurative days. They are compared to the literal work week. Note that this was not simply a memorial day to represent the Sabbath, it was a plan for the work week that God had exemplified in His own creative work.

Ross: "King David in Psalm 95:7-11 also refers to God's seventh day of rest as ongoing." [p. 49]

FALSE. David did not state that the seventh day of Creation continued from the past into the present. David is clearly alluding to rest in the promised land, not Day Seven.

David said, *"Do not harden your hearts, as in the rebellion, As in the day of trial in the wilderness, When your fathers tested Me... For forty years I was grieved with that generation, ...So I swore in My wrath, 'They shall not enter My rest'"* (Psalm 95:8-11, *NKJV*). The people who rebelled against God at Meribah did not receive rest in Canaan; they were forced to wander in the wilderness for 40 years, eventually perishing. David uses this as an illustration of why we should be careful not to let our hearts become hard, and thus require God's discipline. These verses have *nothing* to do with the "rest" of Day Seven.

Also note that the quotation made by David comes from Deuteronomy 12:9, *"For you have not as yet come to the resting place and the inheritance which the Lord your God is giving you"* (*NASB*). This refers specifically to the promised inheritance of the land of Canaan.

Ross: *"Further information about the seventh day is given in ...Hebrews 4 ...we learn that God's day of rest continues."* [p. 49]

FALSE. The writer of Hebrews does not state that the seventh day continues from the past into the present. Like David in Psalms, the writer of Hebrews, is warning the elect not to be disobedient and hard-hearted. Thus, he alludes to Israel in the wilderness who because of their hard hearts could not receive God's promise of rest in Canaan.

---

*For in six days
the Lord made the heavens and the earth,
the sea and all that is in them...*

Exodus 20:11

"Rest," as used in these verses by both David and the writer of Hebrews, had a specific historic reference to the promised land of Canaan. The Hebrew word used by David for "rest" was "menuwchah" which is a general term for rest which has a special *locational* emphasis (e.g., *"the resting place or abode of resting"*). [Francis Brown, et al, *The New Brown-Driver-Briggs-Gesenius Hebrew and English Lexicon* (Peabody, MA: Hendrickson Publishers, 1979), p. 629b] This concept is echoed by the author of Hebrews who uses the Greek word "katapausis" which also may refer to an abode or location of resting (Hebrews 4:1,3-5,8).

At the climax of this passage, the author promises a *future* day of rest (Hebrews 4:9, Greek: "Sabbatismos"). This is the only time in the New Testament that this word for "rest" is employed. It seems to be a deliberate reference to the Day Seven of Creation. The author does not say, however, that the seventh day continues on into the future. He uses "Sabbatismos" without an article (like saying a̲ Sabbath, rather than t̲h̲e̲ Sabbath). In Greek, this grammatical structure would generally represent the character or nature of Day Seven, *without really being Day Seven*. That is, the context makes it clear that the future day of rest will be similar to the original seventh day. The task will be complete; we will live with Christ eternally — our work on earth will be done. [For an excellent analysis of the "rest" offered in Hebrews, see: Thomas Kem Oberholtzer, "The Kingdom Rest in Hebrews 3:1-4:13," *Bibliotheca Sacra* (Dallas, TX: Dallas Theological Seminary, April-June 1988), pp. 185-196).]

CLAIM: Genesis 1 is different than the other chapters, therefore the days can be long.

Creation and Time continues to attempt to convince readers that the word "day" in Genesis 1 should actually be understood as a long, undefined period of time. Ross states that "day" when used with an ordinal modifier in Genesis 1 should not be judged according to the rest of the uses which indicate 24 hour days because Genesis 1 is different than all other chapters. [pp. 46-47]

FALSE. *Creation and Time* makes the old argument that Genesis 1 must be viewed differently than all other Scriptural references. There is no support for this assumption.

Our only hope of understanding the Bible is to interpret Scripture according to sound hermeneutics. The very use of this argument concedes the fact that in every other instance in the Old Testament where day (yom) is used with an ordinal modifier (a number) it represents a normal day. This holds true in at least 358 of the 359 times that day ("yom") is used outside of Genesis 1. (The slightly questionable usage is in Hosea 6:2. See following section.) Also, every instance where day (yom) is modified by "evening and morning" it always represents a normal 24 hour day. This phrase is used 38 times in the Old Testament, not counting Genesis 1. Each time, without exception, the phrase refers to a normal, 24-hour-type day.

In the Creation narrative, the author combines day with *both* an ordinal modifier *and* the phrase *"and there was evening and there was morning"* (Genesis 1:5, etc.). Could God have been any more clear about the nature of the Creation days?!

CLAIM: The Creation days do not have to be literal because not all numbered days in the Bible refer to 24-hour periods.

Dr. Ross proposes that there is one case where "yom" (day) was non-literal when used with a number — Hosea 6:2. *"For centuries Bible commentators have noted that the 'days' in this passage (where the ordinal modifier is used) refer to a year, years, a thousand years, or maybe more."* [p. 47] On this basis, Ross states, *"Neither do numbered days refer strictly to 24-hour periods."* [Hugh Ross, "The Creation-Date Controversy," *The Real Issue* (Dallas, TX: Christian Leadership Ministries, 1994)]

MISLEADING. This conclusion is not well justified. Furthermore, a clear understanding of Hosea 6:2 does not cloud the issue regarding Genesis 1. The Creation days were clearly 24-hour-type days.

Hosea uses a Hebrew idiom in this verse. However, there is no way of understanding the significance of this prophecy if "day" is divorced from its normal meaning of 24 hours. Such a divorce is necessary for Dr. Ross if he is to apply this use to Genesis 1. That is, when reading the word "day" in Genesis 1, Ross does not want the reader to think of a 24-hour day in any sense, even figurative. He desires that the reader understand the word "day" in the sense of "a long period of time."

However, this divorce cannot be made in Hosea 6:2. The prophecy recorded here is a promise by God to restore Israel in a short period of time at some time in the future. It reads, *"He will revive us after two days; He will raise us up on the third day."*

The verse clearly uses a Hebrew idiom *("after two days... on the third day")*. An idiom is a figure of speech that is unique to a particular people or region.

We see, therefore, that if "two days" and "three days" in this idiom do not immediately conjure to mind the period of normal 24-hour-type days, this expression loses its proper figurative meaning (i.e., a very short period of time). Thus, the prophecy of God would lose its significance.

This point is illustrated in other passages which use figurative speech. For example, Psalm 18:2 declares, *"The Lord is my rock"* (*NASB*). The 23rd Psalm compares David to a lamb and says *"the Lord is my shepherd"* (*NASB*). Moses said *"the Lord is my Banner"* (Exodus 17:15, *NASB*). The language is clearly figurative; the Lord *is not actually* a banner, shepherd or rock. The point is this: the reason these figures of speech communicate an effective emotional word-picture is because readers understand the literal meaning of those things to which the Lord is compared. If those literal meanings were removed, the figures of speech would lose their significance.

We know from Moses that the world was not in existence before 6,000 years ago.

Martin Luther

Perhaps this can be made more clear by inventing a meaningless, nonsense word to represent a word of unknown meaning. For example, if a verse were to read, "The Lord is my *zidderzap*, " no one would understand. If Hosea wrote, "He will revive us after two *zidderzaps*; He will raise us up on the third *zidderzap*," the meaning would be a mystery.

For Ross's argument to be effective, the meaning of *zidderzap* in this later case needs to be "long period of time." Otherwise, it cannot be applied as needed to Genesis 1. It does no good if *zidderzap* means a 24-hour-type day. For if Genesis 1:5 reads, even figuratively, as, "So the evening and the morning were the first '24-hour day'," then this figurative use would clearly indicate that the period of time is very short.

Still, one may wonder, if "day" is used figuratively in Hosea 6:2, doesn't that open the door to "day" being figurative in Genesis 1? The answer is clearly, no. There are major differences between the context of these two sections. The Hebrew grammar of Hosea 6:2 plainly shows the passage is meant as a rhetorical device. There are no similar grammatical indications in Genesis 1. On the contrary, the literal meaning of days in Genesis 1 is verified in a straightforward manner.

For a more technical explanation, see the following:

"The collocation of a numeral with the next above it... is a rhetorical device employed in numerical sayings to express a number, which need not, or cannot, be more exactly specified." [E. Kautzsch & A.E. Cowley, *Gesenius' Hebrew Grammar* (New York, NY: Oxford Press, 1990), p. 437]

"By the definition 'after two days,' and 'on the third day,' the speedy and certain revival of Israel is set before them. Two and three days are very short periods of time; and the linking together of two numbers following one upon the other, expresses the certainty of what is to take place... just as in the so-called numerical saying in... [Amos 1:3, Job 5:19, Proverbs 6:16, 30:15,18], *in which the last and greater number expresses the highest or utmost that is generally met with."* [Keil & Delitzsch, *Commentaries on the Old Testament - Minor Prophets*, Vol. 1 (Grand Rapids, MI: Wm. B. Eerdmans Pub. Co., 1971), p. 95]

CLAIM: God could not have used different wording in Genesis 1 to more clearly indicate long "days."

"Young-earthers also hold the view that the Hebrew word 'olam would have been used to indicate a long time period..." [p. 47]

Creation and Time goes on to claim that *"Hebrew lexicons show that only in post-biblical writings did 'olam only refer to a long age or epoch. In biblical time it meant 'forever,' 'perpetual,' 'lasting,'*

'always,' 'of olden times,' or 'the remote past, future, or both.' <u>But</u>
<u>the range of its usage did not include a set period of time.</u>" [p.47 — emphasis added]

FALSE. Dr. Ross's own reference refutes his claim.

He uses *The Theological Wordbook of the Old Testament (TWOT)*
to support his quotes. (Note: *Creation and Time* incorrectly cites Vol. 1 rather
than Vol. 2.) In reality, this reference work shows that 'olam could
have been used if Moses had desired to show long epochs or
ages rather than literal days in Genesis 1. TWOT states, *"There
are at least twenty instances where it clearly refers to the past. Such
usages generally point to something that seems long ago, but rarely if
ever refer to a limitless past... None of these past references has the
idea of endlessness or limitlessness, but each points to a time long
before the immediate knowledge of those living."* [p. 672] Examples of
the references listed in TWOT are: Deuteronomy 32:7, Job
22:15, I Samuel 27:8, Isaiah 51:9; 63:9,11, Genesis 6:4. Certainly,
'olam was used by biblical authors to represent periods of time
in the distant past.

Could 'olam refer to a set period of time? TWOT states, *"The
LXX (Septuagint) generally translates 'olam by aion (Greek) which
has essentially the same range of meaning. That neither the Hebrew
nor the Greek word in itself contains the idea of endlessness is shown
by the fact that they sometimes refer to events or conditions that occurred at a definite point in the past."* [p. 673]

Whether or not 'olam could have been used by an author
intending to show long Creation days, it is apparent that *Creation and Time* misrepresents the sources used to support Ross's
opinion concerning this important matter.

CLAIM: Genesis 1 is a chronology. Therefore, the days were not 24 hours.

Creation and Time claims that Genesis 1 fits the definition of a
"chronology" and then uses the claim to support the Progressive
Creationist long-day view. Ross defines a "chronology" as *"record(ing)
sequences that are both significant and discernible to the reader. The*

timing and order are important because they show the careful unfold-ing of God's plans and affirm his control." [p. 47]

The book gives several examples of what Ross classifies as chro-nologies. It concludes that *"the creation days, long time periods dur-ing which increasingly complex life-forms were created, indeed, are verifiable and essential to validate the supernatural accuracy of the writer's statements. But if all creation were completed in six twenty-four hour days, the most sophisticated measuring techniques avail-able... would be totally incapable of discerning the sequence of events. Thus a major use of the chronology would be thwarted."* [p. 48]

FALSE. This is a meaningless argument formed without bibli-cal basis.

1. It is noteworthy that Ross provides his own definition for a "chronology" because none exists in biblical scholarship.

2. *Creation and Time* fails to reference support on this topic, which suggests that the classification of a "chronology" exists only in Ross's mind.

3. Ross's examples of chronologies all deal with *future* events (Jeremiah 31:38-40, Daniel 9:24-27, 11:2-35). Admittedly, verification of prophecies was extremely important. How-ever, none of the "chronologies" cited refers to *past* events such as the Creation Week. To classify the Creation account as a "chronology" is unwarranted and meaningless.

It appears that Dr. Ross has invented his own classification and then created his own definition. Thus, it is no surprise that an old-earth "evidence" results from this interpretation.

CLAIM: Because Adam used the word "happa'am" when he saw Eve, the 6th day was a long period.

When Adam first saw Eve, he exclaimed, "This is now [happa'am in Hebrew] bone of my bones and flesh of my flesh; she shall be called 'woman,' for she was taken out of man." *Creation and Time* claims this phrase shows that the 6th day of Creation was a very long period of time. He says, *"This expression is underline{usually} translated as 'now at length' (see Genesis 29:34-35, 30:20, 46:30; Judges 15:3), roughly equivalent to our English expression 'at last'."* [p. 51 — emphasis added]

> FALSE. Not only is *Creation and Time's* interpretation of this word wrong, but so is its claim that "now at length" is the usual translation.
>
> *Creation and Time* states that "happa'am" is "usually translated as 'now at length'." It is revealing to note that contrary to this claim, none of the major Bible versions use Ross's phrases "at long last" or "now at length" in their translation — not the *King James Version, New King James Version, New International Version,* or the *New American Standard Bible.* Not one of the major, respected Bible translations uses a phrase consistent with Ross's claim. One wonders if he actually looked up the referenced verses.
>
> "Happaam" is actually the word "paam" with the article attached. "Paam" has several meanings, depending upon its context. The definitive book *Gesenius' Hebrew Grammar* confirms that when "paam" is connected with the article, the appropriate meaning is "this time." In fact, this verse (Genesis 2:23) is the example that is used for this grammatical rule. [*Gesenius' Hebrew Grammar*, Second Edition, edited and enlarged by E. Kautzsch and revised by A.E. Cowley (Great Britain: Oxford University Press, 1910), p. 404]
>
> The intended meaning of "this time" makes perfect sense considering the context. Adam had been assigned the task of naming animals so that he could understand his own need for a helper. One after another, the pairs paraded past. *"But for Adam there was not found a helper suitable for him"* (Genesis 2:20, *NASB*). Then the Lord placed Adam into a deep sleep and removed a portion of his side with which Eve was created. When the woman was brought to Adam, he exclaimed, *"This one, this time, is bone of my bones, and flesh of my flesh..."* (Genesis 2:23, literal Hebrew). It is as if Adam is saying, this time I have found the one suitable to be my helper!

CLAIM: The events of the sixth day prove that it must have been longer than a normal day.

Ross: *"The events between Adam's creation and Eve's seem to require far more than 24 hours."* [Hugh Ross, "The Creation-Date Controversy," *The Real Issue* (Dallas, TX: Christian Leadership Ministries, 1994)] For Dr. Ross, it seems the biggest problem would have involved Adam's *"assignment from God to name all the animals (the nephesh creatures - i.e., all the birds and mammals)."* [p. 51]

FALSE. Not only does Genesis not say that Adam named all the animals, but Dr. Ross fails to understand the implications of God's purpose in bringing them to Adam. In reality, the events of Day Six produce a far larger problem for Progressive Creationists than they do for young-earth creationists.

Here is what the main verses involved say, *"Now the LORD God had formed out of the ground all the beasts of the field and all the birds of the air. He brought them to the man to see what he would name them; and whatever the man called each living creature, that was its name. So <u>the man gave names to all the livestock, the birds of the air and all the beasts of the field</u>. But for Adam no suitable helper was found"* (Genesis 2:19-20, *NIV* — emphasis added).

- THE BIBLE DOES NOT SAY THAT ADAM NAMED ALL THE ANIMALS or all the birds and mammals. Thus, Dr. Ross's first error is in his claim that God commanded Adam to *"name <u>all</u> the animals (the nephesh creatures - i.e., <u>all</u> the birds and mammals.)"* [p. 51 — emphasis added] A smaller group of animals was involved: livestock, *flying* birds, and beasts of the *field* (Genesis 2:20). Note that Adam was told to name the beasts-of-the-*fields*, not beasts-of-the-*earth* (evidently the field-beasts were a sub-set of the larger category, beasts-of-the-*earth* — Genesis 1:24-25). Various commentators agree that these field-beasts were animals that lived in or near the Garden. Other animals were also excluded from this initial naming event. These include the fish, water-dwelling mammals, and *"creatures that move along the ground"* (Genesis 1:24, *NIV*), including most reptiles, insects and many of the small mammals. Thus, a very large number of animals are eliminated from naming on Day Six.

- HOW MANY ANIMALS WERE INVOLVED IN THIS LESSER GROUP? Dr. Henry Morris suggests perhaps 3,000 kinds. [Henry M. Morris, *The Genesis Record* (Grand Rapids, MI: Baker Book House, 1976), p. 97] Dr. Ross assumes a far larger number. However, it is interesting to note that not all Progressive Creationists agree with Ross on this point. For example, theologian Dr. Gleason Archer estimated that *"many hun-dreds of species must have been involved"* in the original creation, not thousands as others propose. [Gleason L. Archer, Jr., in *Hermeneutics, Inerrancy and the Bible*, edited by Earl Radmacher and Robert Preus (Grand Rapids, MI: Zondervan Publishing House, 1984), p. 326 — emphasis added] It should be noted that the modern term "species" is foreign to the context of the Bible. Genesis tells us that God created every animal according to its own "kind." It is probable that there were far fewer "kinds" at the time of Creation than there are "species" today. Progressive Creationist Walter Bradley agrees that *"God created the major types of animals and plant life and then used process to develop the tremendous variety of life forms we observe today."* [Walter L. Bradley in *Hermeneutics, Inerrancy and the Bible*, edited by Earl Radmacher and Robert Preus (Grand Rapids, MI: Zondervan Publishing House, 1984), p. 290 — emphasis added] How many animal kinds were in this lesser group? It is impossible to know.

- "ALL" , DOES NOT NECESSARILY MEAN EACH AND EVERY. Hebrew grammars and lexicons demonstrate that the word "all" can have numerous applications and points of emphasis. The Bible sometimes uses "all" when referring to "each and every" member of the modified subject, as in Romans 3:23: *"All have sinned and fall short of the glory of God"* (*NASB*). In this case, it is obvious that "all" refers to every human who has ever existed — each and every person. However, concerning John the Baptist, the Bible uses "all" differently. *"Then Jerusalem was going out to him, and all Judea, and all the district around the Jordan"* (Matthew 3:5, *NASB*). In this case, few would argue that "all" refers to each and every man, woman and child. Thus we find that "all" may be used in many different ways in Hebrew and Greek, just as in English. Within the syntax of Genesis 2:20, we note that the author uses "all" with singular nouns ("cattle" and "beast"). Various Hebrew scholars confirm that this construction emphasizes the collective usage of the noun, rather than each individual in that category. This argument does not deny that group categories are made up of individual kinds of animals, yet it is the collective nature of these categories which is emphasized. [*Gesenius' Hebrew Grammar*, pp. 410-11 (127b-c); Francis Brown, et al, *The New Brown-Driver-Briggs-Gesenius Hebrew and English Lexicon* (Peabody, MA: Hendrickson Publishers, 1979), p. 481] Therefore, it seems reasonable to conclude that in Genesis 2:20, "all" could refer to the collective nature of God's creation. Thus, Adam would only have named the number of animals required to fulfill God's purpose for this task.

- WHAT WAS THE PURPOSE OF ADAM'S TASK? The main purpose seems to make Adam discover his unique aloneness. He was the only one without a mate. This is suggested by the entire context of these verses. The naming process was surely not meant to be a lesson in taxonomy. Nor does it seem probable that Adam named the animals because they immediately needed names for identification. Neither did God bring the animals to Adam to temporarily eliminate any feelings of loneliness. The Bible emphasizes that the main point of this lesson was learned by Adam, *"but for Adam there was not found a helper suitable for him"* (Genesis 2:20, *NASB*).

- UNDERSTANDING THE PURPOSE, HOW MUCH TIME WAS NECESSARY? Understanding the purpose of this naming exercise is important to estimating how long the process might have taken. The number of animals would be determined by how long it would take Adam to fully get the point. Since Adam was created in God's image, the image of One who communicates and shares in loving relationships, it seems doubtful that Adam would have needed years, months, weeks, or even days to understand the importance of companionship. It is probable that Adam, placed in the midst of such an excellent illustration, would have realized his own need for a helper in only a matter of hours.

Dr. Ross objects that too many things happened on Day Six for it to be a normal length day. [pp. 50-51]

What events does Genesis 1-2 list for Day Six?

1. God created livestock, beasts of the earth, and everything that creeps on the earth.
2. God created Adam.
3. God planted the Garden.
4. God talked to Adam.
5. God brought certain animals to Adam.
6. Adam named animals
7. God created Eve.

We find no reason to doubt that these events could all have happened during a normal 24 hour day. Our all-powerful Creator is easily capable of doing far, far more than this in 24 hours. He said that He did these things in a single day, and we believe Him.

The Sixth Day problem for Progressive Creationism

Although the events of Day Six are no problem for young-earth creationists, they are virtually impossible for Progressive Creationists:

1. TOO MANY ANIMALS OVER ENORMOUS AREAS, SEPARATED BY VAST OCEANS. Ross claims that Adam was commanded to name all of the nephesh animals, which he claims consists of *all* the birds and mammals. According to his own teachings, animals lived all around the world and on each of today's continents. How then was Adam to name *all* the animals, particularly since some were unique to specific continents? It would be nearly impossible for Adam to get to the animals over such vast spaces separated by oceans, let alone name such a huge number.

2. ROSS'S "METICULOUS" ADAM WOULD BE EVEN WORSE OFF. Dr. Ross claims that *"Adam in his perfect state would be all the more meticulous in performing his God-assigned tasks."* [p.51] In other words, rather than speeding Adam, his sin-free body, brain and mind would supposedly slow him down. Ross implies that Adam had to meticulously

analyze each creature before naming it. If all the animals on each continent had to be named, the task becomes Herculean. Even if Adam was asked to name just the animals in his part of the world, such a task would surely take a lifetime, not just a few years. Clearly such a period and process are not implied from the biblical text.

3. WHY KEEP ADAM LONELY FOR SO LONG? Even if Adam took a minimum time of a few years (it is hard to imagine any shorter time given Ross's interpretation of the text), how are we to understand such an illogical assignment from God? The Creator said, *"It is not good for the man to be alone..."* (Genesis 2:18, *NASB*). Why would God require Adam to live "alone" in a condition that was "not good" for so long? This is not the kind of God we know.

CONCLUSION. Dr. Ross argues that the events of the sixth day could not be accomplished in a normal 24 hour period. This does not stand up to biblical investigation. We must not make the text say more than it actually says. When we take the meaning from the text (rather than reading current ideas into the text), there is no reason to doubt that all of the events of Day Six occurred during a normal length day.

CLAIM: The Hebrew word "toledah" (Genesis 2:4) indicates old universe.

Genesis 2:4 says, "These are the generations of the heavens and of the earth when they were created" (KJV). Dr. Ross writes, *"Hebrew lexicons verify that the word for generation (toledah) refers to the time between a person's birth and parenthood or to an arbitrarily longer time span. In Genesis 2:4 the plural form, generations, is used, indicating that multiple generations have passed."* [p. 52] Dr. Ross supports his views by a reference to the *Theological Wordbook of the Old Testament (TWOT)*.

FALSE. Dr. Ross is incorrect about the meaning of the Hebrew word "toledah" and his support material says the exact opposite of what he claims.

First, as to the translation that Dr. Ross gives for the Hebrew word "toledot", (Note: *TWOT*, which Ross claims as support, references this word as "toledot", not "toledah") The *Theological Wordbook of the Old Testament* states, "*The common translation as 'generations' does not convey the meaning of the word to modern readers... As used in the OT, toledot refers to what is produced or brought into being by someone, or follows therefrom.*" Ross's claim that this Hebrew word refers to the time between a person's birth and parenthood is without support and is contradicted by the very Lexicon he references!

Second, Ross states that "*In Genesis 2:4 the plural form, generations, is used, indicating multiple generations have passed.*" [p. 52] Again, Dr. Ross contradicts the very Lexicon which he uses as support. *TWOT* says "*It (toledot) occurs only in the plural, and only in the construct state or with a pronominal suffix.*" In other words, the "singular" form of toledot does not exist in biblical literature. Therefore, Ross's argument for multiple generations is without support and is contradicted by the very Lexicon he references!

If the Bible is God's Word (as it repeatedly claims),
and if Ross's Progressive Creationism is true
(local Flood —
Creation days which are overlapping eons —
death, disease, and degeneration before Adam —
no humans until the last moment of billions-of-years),
then God has been deceptive.

Having established that the *TWOT* does not support the claims of *Creation and Time*, the question may be asked, "What does the Lexicon say regarding the use of toledot in Genesis 2:4?" *TWOT* states, "*It is reasonable to translate Genesis 2:4, 'These are the toledot of heaven and earth,' as meaning, not the coming of heaven and earth into existence, but the events that followed the establishment of heaven and earth. Thus the verse is correctly placed as introducing the detailed account of the creation and fall of man. It is not a summary of the event preceding Genesis 2:4.*"

The *Theological Wordbook of the Old Testament* (Vol. 1, p. 378-380) shows that the way Dr. Ross uses the Hebrew word "toledot" as evidence for an old universe and earth is in terrible error. Dr. Ross has misunderstood this important argument and has misrepresented *TWOT's* support of his views.

Hebrew words — more examples of inaccurate claims for their meaning

CLAIM: Nephesh = birds and mammals

Creation and Time states that the Hebrew word "nephesh" represents *"soulish creatures, creatures that can relate to humans; creatures with qualities of mind, will, and emotion. These can only be birds and mammals."* [p. 152 — emphasis added]

FALSE. This statement is incorrect. Nephesh does not refer to only birds and mammals. Nephesh clearly has a wide range of usage. It is basically the Hebrew word for "life."

Creation and Time does not reference its source of information for his unorthodox interpretation. Had Ross looked at one of his favorite lexicons, *The Theological Wordbook of the Old Testament*, he could have noted the true meaning. "Nephesh" is generally used for "life" or "soul" ("soul, but not in the New Testament sense of spiritual but rather as a whole living being") [Vol. 2, p. 590].

In Genesis 1:21 nephesh is used as a general term for water animals, in Genesis 1:24 it is used with land animals, and in Genesis 2:7 it is used with humans. The *Theological Wordbook* makes no mention of nephesh meaning "soulish creatures" or "mammals."

Why is it important for Dr. Ross to translate this and some of the following Hebrew words for animals in a new way? It is part of an attempt to harmonize a conflict between Scripture and Ross's understanding of the fossil record with its timeline which is shared with the evolutionists. The biblical order of

Creation flatly contradicts the secular timeline in several instances.

In response, Creation and Time *claims that "the few purported conflicts with the fossil record stem from inaccurate interpretations of some Hebrew nouns for various plant and animal species." (p. 151)*

It appears the author is primarily trying to solve the well-known conflicts between the order of Creation in Genesis and the order of appearance of plants and animals accepted by secular science (single-celled creatures / fish / amphibians / reptiles / birds and mammals). The following table illustrates the situation.

GENESIS SAYS	SECULAR SCIENCE SAYS
Reptiles (6th Day) were created AFTER birds (5th Day).	Reptiles came BEFORE birds.
Insects (included in "creeping things" — 6th Day) were created AFTER birds (5th Day).	Insects came long BEFORE the first birds.
Birds and fishes created at the same time (5th day).	Fishes came hundreds of millions of years BEFORE birds.
Fish and other sea animals (5th Day) were created AFTER fruit trees and other land plants (3rd Day).	The first living things were sea creatures. The first fish came long BEFORE the first fruit trees.
Land mammals (6th Day) were created AFTER whales and other sea mammals (5th Day).	Whales and other sea mammals came long AFTER the first land mammals.
Insects (6th Day) were created AFTER plants (3rd Day).	Flowering plants and pollinating insects evolved (or were created) simultaneously for their mutual benefit. Few flowering plants could survive without insects for pollination.

The biblical record obviously contradicts secular science's interpretation of the fossil record. In an effort at harmonization, in order to justify his Progressive Creation stand, Dr. Ross makes some major misinterpretations of Hebrew words. If he were to acknowledge the error in his Hebrew translations, he would be forced to fall back on his final line of defense — claiming that the Creation days actually overlapped each other.

In another publication, Dr. Ross provides a graph illustrating his theory. In defense of the concept, Ross simply states, *"To insist that the creation events of Genesis must be specifically limited to the creation days in which they are mentioned is to read too much into the text."* [Hugh Ross, "Genesis One: A Scientific Perspective," (Sierra Madre, CA: Wisemen Productions, 1983), p. 12 — emphasis added]

FALSE. This bold claim is not defended by Ross with biblical evidence — and for good reason; there is none. In context, the concept is nonsensical. Genesis 1 clearly gives the very distinct impression that God performed separate, unique creations on distinct and consecutive days. True, God didn't say "and I do mean *all* birds" at the end of the 4th day, for example. But this hardly seems necessary.

Ross's theory (as illustrated by his graph):

- Some PLANTS were created during Days 2, 4 and 5, even though God clearly gave the impression that Day 3 was uniquely set aside for this task.

- Some SEA CREATURES and BIRDS were actually created during Days 3, 4 and 6, even though Genesis ascribes them to Day 5.

- Some CREATURES THAT MOVE ALONG THE GROUND and WILD ANIMALS were created on Days 4 and 5, despite Genesis' description placing them on Day 6.

Is the biblical description of daily events really this meaningless?!? God divided the creative process into six days — and consecutively numbered each day — and repeatedly stated that each had a distinct beginning and end ("evening and morning"). This certainly gives the impression of consecutive days! If the days are overlapping, as Dr. Ross describes, it appears that God has been deceptive — misleading readers with these specifics. In other words, the meaning which was taken as obvious (and remained undoubted) by Christians and Jews for centuries was wrong. It is not hard to see that this is a very weak argument indeed.

Combined with Dr. Ross's inaccurate Hebrew word studies, this leaves him faced with a major contradiction. He needs to decide whether to support the order of events espoused by secular science or the clear order of Creation described in Genesis 1. Harmonization is not possible. God, Himself, prevented it — and for good reason.

People need to understand that
God created a wonderful paradise and
that suffering, death and evil came into the world
through Adam's sin.

CLAIM: Chayyah = long-legged, wild quadruped

Creation and Time claims that the "chayyah" is a mammal; a *"long-legged quadruped usually described as wild."* [p. 152]

FALSE. Chayyah can refer to many types of living creatures.

Once again, Dr. Ross bases his argument that the "chayyah" are mammals because of their association with "nephesh" (living). This interpretation is in error. The *Theological Wordbook of the Old Testament* states that *"the term is used mostly of wild animals in contrast to domestic animals. Psalm 104:25 uses it of creatures that live in water. Ezekiel in chapter 1 employs the term to describe the 'living creatures' of his vision."* [Vol. 1, p. 281] We note therefore that "chayyah" can refer to all types of living creatures, not simply wild mammals.

Of special interest to this issue is Leviticus 11:9-12. These verses give the Jewish people prohibitions to certain types of food. In this case, only fish that have both fins and scales could be eaten. This ruled out eels, shellfish, lobsters, crabs, oysters, etc. It is interesting that "chayyah nephesh" is used in verse 10 to refer to all the living creatures in the waters. Certainly these terms do not refer to all the wild, long-legged, mammalian quadrupeds that lived in the water. No, these terms (just as the others investigated) have a much broader usage than that given by *Creation and Time*.

CLAIM: Behema = long-legged, domestic mammals

Creation and Time claims that "behema" is a mammal and refers only to a *"long-legged quadruped that is easy to tame."* [p. 152]

FALSE. Behema can refer to almost any animal, including "wild" animals.

The *Theological Wordbook of the Old Testament* says that *"behema can refer to both wild beast, though exclusive use as wild beast is less frequent, and domestic animals. When referring to domestic animals, behema usually includes both large cattle and sheep, but not the 'creeping things.'"* [Vol. 1, p. 92] Again we notice that the neat little categories set up by Dr. Ross to support his view of Creation do not work.

While behema often refers to domestic animals, it also refers to all animals, including those classified by the modern term "wild." We also see once again that behema need not be thought of as a mammal. *Creation and Time* makes this conclusion based upon a false assumption concerning the word nephesh, as seen above.

CLAIM: Remes = short-legged land mammals (in Genesis 1)

Creation and Time teaches that the Hebrew word "remes" in a *"broad definition encompasses rapidly moving vertebrates, such as rodents, hares, and lizards. But remes in verse 24 (Gen. 1) has a more restricted usage. The creatures under discussion are the nephesh - soulish creatures... so remes of verse 24 cannot be insects or even reptiles. They must be short-legged land mammals such as rodents and hares."* [p. 152]

FALSE. Remes in Genesis 1 could refer to insects and reptiles, mammals and almost any small, living creatures.

The *Theological Wordbook of the Old Testament* states that "*Remes means not only small mammals such as rodents but the small reptiles common in the gravel and rocks of Palestine.*" [Vol. 2, p. 850] It also states remes is, "*The Hebrew verb which describes the locomotion of small animals, especially reptiles. It appears primarily in the account of creation, and in the prohibition against unclean foods.*" TWOT makes no mention of exceptions to these definitions.

Creation and Time basically agrees with these definitions but argues that because these "remes" are "nephesh" that they must be mammals. This is based upon a misunderstanding of the word nephesh, as shown previously. The creation of "remes" in Genesis 1 certainly could refer to insects, reptiles and small mammals — in other words, small living creatures.

In light of *Creation and Time's* claims about these Hebrew nouns for animals, Leviticus 11 contains an important verse to study. It demonstrates the way that these common Hebrew words are used in a general manner — not specifying species or phyla. Leviticus 11:46 — "*These are the regulations concerning animals* [behema], *birds, every living thing* [chayyah nephesh] *that moves* [remes] *in the water and every creature* [nephesh] *that moves about on the ground*" (*NIV*). Investigation of the Hebrew words "nephesh, remes, behema and chayyah" show that *Creation and Time* has mistranslated each — evidently based upon a preconceived notion that the biblical narrative of Creation must be harmonized with secular science's interpretation of the geologic column.

...since sin entered the stream of history man has...
perverted, blunted, diluted, and corrupted that
which was originally true truth that did come from God.
For us today the only infallible canon
for determining true truth is the written Word of God.
Nature... is limited and can be misread by mankind.

Dr. Charles Ryrie

History of Creationism

CLAIM: The early Church Fathers supported long Creation days.

Ross: *"Many Christians have been taught that through the first seventeen centuries of the church, until the industrial revolution and the scientific age, there was general agreement on the six-twenty-four-hour-creation-days interpretation. But this is not what the literature shows."* [p. 16] *Creation and Time* states, *"A majority of those who wrote on the subject rejected the concrete interpretation of the Genesis creation days as six consecutive twenty-four-hour periods."* [p. 24 — emphasis added] Dr. Ross further claims that a great many of the leaders of the early church did not believe that the Creation Week consisted of literal days. [Chapter 2, pp. 16-24] Those "Church Fathers" named in *Creation and Time* as evidence for this view are: (1) Philo, (2) Josephus, (3) Justin Martyr, (4) Irenaeus, (5) Hippolytus, (6) Ambrose, (7) Clement of Alexandria, (8) Origen, (9) Lactantius, (10) Victorinus of Pettau, (11) Methodius of Olympus, (12) Augustine, (13) Eusebius, and (14) Basil. [pp. 16-24]

FALSE. Most of the Church Fathers that Ross lists supported literal days. Do the following quotations from these Church Fathers sound like the writings of men who believed in figurative Creation days?

Ambrose (c. AD 340-397) wrote in his address known as the Hexameron, *"Scripture established a law that twenty-four hours, including both day and night, should be given the name of day only, as if one were to say the length of one day is twenty-four hours in extent... God commanded that the heavens should come into existence, and it was done; He determined that the earth should be created, and it was created... These things were made in a moment."* [*The Nicene & Post Nicene Fathers*, Vol. 10, pp. 187-188 — emphasis added]

Victorinus of Pettau (later third century) wrote, *"even such is the rapidity of that creation; as is contained in the book of Moses, which he wrote about its creation, and which is called Genesis. God produced that entire mass for the adornment of His majesty in six days; on the seventh to which He consecrated it and blessed it. ...In the beginning God made the light, and divided it into the exact measure of twelve hours by day and by night."* ["On the Creation of the World," *Ante Nicene Fathers*, Vol. 7, p. 341 — emphasis added]

One is caused to question whether Dr. Ross has actually read any of the writings he quotes. Most of the "Church Fathers" he claims as believing in figurative "days" actually believed just the opposite. This is even evident within the same context of the quotes Ross reported. *Creation and Time* misinterprets no fewer than 9 of the 14 men listed. We feel that the following table more accurately expresses the beliefs of these men.

It is both interesting and important to note that the only men on Ross's list who actually may have expressed doubts about *"the concrete interpretation of the Genesis creation days as consecutive twenty-four-hour periods"* [p. 24] are those from the Alexandrian school of theology. These men favored allegorization of all types, involving far more than just the days of Genesis.

The school of Alexandria was founded by Clement in an attempt to harmonize the teachings of the Bible with the "truths" of Greek philosophy. The peculiar, unorthodox theological views of the Alexandrian allegorists such as Clement and Origen are well-known to evangelical scholars. These men had a strong tendency to heavily allegorize much of Scripture. Their interpretations denied or de-emphasized the literal, historical aspect of the various narratives in favor of mystical, "spiritual," allegorical interpretations.

Although Origen was a dedicated Christian and prolific author, he was controversial even in his own time due to various personal views. He was the greatest allegorizer of all. For example, Origen denied hell, teaching that everyone would eventually be saved, even Satan and his demons. His views

MORE ACCURATE LISTING OF CHURCH FATHERS

Believed in literal days	View unclear (their writings do not address the topic)	Alexandrian school (believed in figurative days)
Justin Martyr (definite)	Hippolytus	Philo (definite; a Jew, not a Church Father; position on ancient earth unclear)
Irenaeus (very likely)	Eusebius	Clement of Alexandria (likely; position on ancient earth unclear)
Lactantius (definite)		Origen (possibly; did not believe in an ancient earth)
Augustine (probable; believed in young earth)		
Victorinus of Pettau (definite)		
Methodius of Olympus (definite)		
Basil (definite)		
Ambrose (definite)		
Theophilus of Antioch (definite)		
Martin of Braga (definite)		
Josephus (very likely; a Jewish historian, not a Church Father)		

were a precursor to various wrong doctrines and heresies. He denied the physical reality of the whole Creation account. He taught that the Garden of Eden, the Tree of Life, the Tree of the Knowledge of Good and Evil, and the serpent did not physically exist. They were fictional stories used to teach moral truths. Considering Origen's record, it does not really matter what he believed about the Creation days.

After Clement's death, Origen became the leader of the Alexandrian school and a highly influential teacher, ultimately influencing the writings of Augustine.

NOTES ON AUGUSTINE, JOSEPHUS, ORIGEN

AUGUSTINE

Because Augustine did allegorize the Creation story, an element of doubt was introduced about his position on the length of the Creation days. However, our research strongly indicates that he accepted literal days. Unfortunately, he seems to have been misinterpreted by evolutionists and some creationists who mistakenly assumed that he believed in long days and evolution. It appears that Augustine was taken out of context and that his use of allegory was misunderstood as anti-historical. Some have even accused Augustine of saying that the days of Creation were 1000 years long. But neither we nor researcher Weston Fields have been able to find any such statement in Augustine's many writings on Creation. [Weston J. Fields, *Unformed and Unfilled* (Nutley, New Jersey: Presbyterian and Reformed Publishing Company, 1976), p. 27]

Although Augustine was a follower of the Alexandrian school, he was much more conservative than Origen. Despite the fact that Augustine looked for the allegorical meanings in biblical texts, including the Creation account, he also accepted the literal stories as historically accurate. He simply looked for other, deeper meanings as well.

A close examination of Augustine's writings reveals various evidences that he probably accepted literal Creation days and a young earth:

1. EVENING AND MORNING. Augustine, in defending the literal resurrection of Jesus on the 3rd day: *"No Christian doubts that the Lord arose from the dead on the third day. Moreover, the holy gospel attests that the Resurrection took place on this night. Furthermore, there is no doubt that the day is computed from the preceding night, and not according to the order of days which is mentioned in Genesis, although there, too, darkness took precedence, for 'darkness covered the abyss,' when 'God said, Let there be light, and there was light.' But because* that darkness was not yet night, for not yet had day come into being, *'God separated the light from the darkness,' first calling the light Day, and then calling the darkness Night. Thus,* the period from the creation of light to another morning was reckoned as one day. It is clear that those days began at dawn and ended at the expiration of night, with the dawn of the next morning.*" [Augustine, "Sermons on the Liturgical Seasons," in *The Fathers of the Church*, 38, translated by Mary Sarah Muldowney (New York: Fathers of the Church, Inc., 1959), pp. 177-178, emphasis added — as cited in Weston J. Fields, *Unformed and Unfilled* (Nutley, New Jersey: Presbyterian and Reformed Publishing Company, 1976), pp. 27-28]

2. BELIEVED EARTH CREATED SIMULTANEOUSLY WITH TIME. Augustine: *"I do not see how He an be said to have created the world after spaces of time had elapsed, ...*assuredly the world was made, not in time, but simultaneously with time. *...in the world's creation change and motion were created, as seems evident from the order of the first six or seven days. For in these days the morning and evening are counted, until, on the sixth day, all things which God then made were finished, and on the seventh the rest of God was mysteriously and sublimely singalized."* [Augustine, The City of God, Book 11, Chapter 6] In other words, both the heavens and the earth were created at the same moment as time began, not long after time began. Ross claims the heavens came billions of years before the earth.

3. LUMINARIES ON THE 4TH DAY. Augustine believed that the sun, moon and stars were created on the 4th day of Creation. This he does not allegorize. *"But the first three days of all were passed without sun, since it is reported to have been made on the fourth day."* [Augustine, *The City of God*, Book 11, chapter 7]

4. ACCEPTS EXISTENCE OF A SUPERNATURAL LIGHT SOURCE ON DAY 1 BEFORE THE SUN'S CREATION ON DAY 4. Augustine unhesitatingly accepted that there was separation of light and dark on Day 1 before the creation of sun, moon and stars on Day 4. *"But what kind of light that was, and by what periodic movement it made evening and morning, is beyond the reach of our senses [he did not know that the earth revolves]; neither can we understand how it was, and <u>yet must unhesitatingly believe it</u>."* [Augustine, *The City of God*, Book 11, chapter 7 — emphasis added] He goes on to add an allegorical interpretation to these "days" of Creation. However, it must be emphasized that an allegorical interpretation does not necessarily negate belief in a historical interpretation. Origen and Augustine would often teach that there were many depths of truths in the Scripture. Some truths were to be found in the historical genre, some in the spiritual. It seems that this may have been a time when Augustine was simply digging for deeper meaning in the Creation narrative.

5. NO HUMAN DEATH BEFORE ADAM. Augustine clearly teaches that humans would not have experienced death if they had not sinned. *"<u>For the first men would not have suffered death had they not sinned</u>... Wherefore we must say that the first men were indeed so created, that if they had not sinned, they would not have experienced any kind of death."* [Augustine, The City of God, Book 13, chapter 3, also see chapter 1 — emphasis added]

6. MAN DID NOT EVOLVE FROM ANIMALS. Augustine does not appear to believe that humans evolved from lower creatures. He states that it pleased God to *"derive <u>all men from one individual,</u> and created man with such a nature that the members of the race <u>should not have died,</u> had not the two first (of whom the one was created out of nothing, and the other out of him) merited this by their disobedience; for by them so great a sin was committed, that by it <u>the human nature was altered</u> for the worse, and was transmitted also to their posterity, liable to sin and subject to death."* [Augustine in *The City of God*, as cited by Norman Geisler in *What Augustine Says* (Grand Rapids, MI: Baker Book House, 1982), p. 119 — emphasis added]

JOSEPHUS

We can find no reason to believe that Josephus rejected literal days. It is clear that he would not agree with Ross's beliefs about days 1, 4 and 7. Josephus certainly accepts that the luminaries were created on the 4th day, not the 1st, and that the 7th day is ended.

In his book of *The Antiquities of the Jews*, Josephus describes Creation as having taken place in six days. He states that the sun, moon and stars were created on the 4th day and that the 7th day of God's rest is a past event with a morning and evening. [Josephus, *Antiquities of the Jews*, Book 1, Chapter 1]

However, referring to the first day, Josephus wrote: *"But Moses said it was one day, the cause of which I am able to give even now; but because I have promised to give such reasons for all things in a treatise by itself, I shall put off its exposition till that time."* [Josephus, *Antiquities of the Jews*, Book 1, Chapter 1]

Josephus never explained this comment. Because of this single sentence, some have suggested (probably wrongly) that Josephus did not believe in literal Creation days. A more likely explanation is that Josephus was not questioning the length of days, but was merely saying that he felt he knew the reason Moses used the term "one day" in Genesis 1:5. The Hebrew literally says "one day," rather than "the first day." The question of why it says "one day" in Genesis 1:5, but "2nd day," "3rd day," and so on in all the other Creation day verses was discussed by several church writers in following centuries. This topic had nothing to do with the acceptance of literal days.

ORIGEN

Origen did not believe in an old earth. For example, he said, *"...this world had its beginning at a certain time, and that agreeably to our belief in Scripture, we can calculate the years of its past duration."* [Origen, "De Principiis," Book 3, Chapter 5, *Ante-Nicene Fathers*, Vol. 4, edited by Roberts & Donaldson (Grand Rapids, MI: WM. B. Eerdmans Pub. Co., 1981), p. 341 — emphasis added]

He also believed that the world and time began simultaneously. In other words, time and the universe did not begin billions of years before earth's creation. Origen: *"...this world was created and took its beginning at a certain time, ...all visible things were created at a certain time."* [Origen, "De Principiis," Book 3, Chapter 5, *Ante-Nicene Fathers*, Vol. 4, edited by Roberts & Donaldson (Grand Rapids, MI: WM. B. Eerdmans Pub. Co., 1981), pp. 340-341]

CLAIM: Even those Church Fathers who did not write about this subject rejected 24 hour days.

Dr. Ross states, *"Perhaps most significant is that nearly all the key figures acknowledged that the length of Genesis creation days presented a challenge to their understanding and interpretation. Those who did not, implied the same in their studious avoidance of any specific comment on the subject."* [p. 24 — emphasis added]

MISLEADING. The opposite appears to be the case.

Creation and Time gives the impression that those who did not happen to address the subject of the length of Creation actually rejected the view of six 24 hour days. Thus, Dr. Ross claims support from all the church leaders who never even addressed this issue! *Creation and Time* is incorrect in its claim that "all the key figures" considered this a challenge. In fact, nearly all the ancient leaders who wrote on the subject take a clear stand for normal, 24 hour days!

Creation and Time suggests that the silence of the remaining Church Fathers endorses Dr. Ross's view. This is unlikely. It is more probable that church leaders didn't write about this issue because it wasn't controversial within their culture. They were busy dealing with heresies concerning the trinity, the incarnation of Christ, the nature of Christ's deity, etc.

The fact that there are very few writings about the length of Creation days tells us that there was a basic agreement among the leaders at that time. What did the leaders believe? Overwhelmingly they show support of Creation within six 24 hour days, and they accept the genealogy from Adam to Christ!

CLAIM: Church scholars of the Dark and Middle Ages would probably also disagree with literal days.

"Throughout the Dark and Middle Ages, church scholars maintained the tolerant attitude of their forefathers toward differing views and interpretations of the creation time scale." [p. 25]

FALSE. This is a groundless and meaningless claim.

Creation and Time provides no proof for this statement. In fact, Ross does not quote from any church leaders during this period. If anything is noteworthy during this portion of church history, certainly it would be the intolerance that existed for those who opposed the official teachings of the church. We have found no reason to believe that there was any serious consideration of any belief other than a literal six day Creation several thousand years before.

CLAIM: Lightfoot and Ussher ignored Hebrew scholarship.

Creation and Time states that Dr. John Lightfoot and Archbishop Ussher were incorrect concerning their Creation dates because *"Both Lightfoot and Ussher ignored Hebrew scholarship."* [p. 26] It further asserts that *"they also assumed, based on the wording of the King James Version, that the numbered days of the Genesis creation account could only be six consecutive twenty-four-hour periods."* [p. 27]

FALSE. Both men were outstanding experts in Hebrew!

Creation and Time belittles these men, and all who would agree with their work, because of their attempts to correctly understand the timing of the Creation event. It wrongly claims that these men of God were ignorant of Hebrew scholarship and led astray by the English translation of the King James Version Bible.

Dr. Adam Clark, author of the best known biography on John Lightfoot said, *"In biblical criticism I consider Lightfoot the first of all English writers; and in this I include his learning, his judgment and his usefulness."* Lightfoot was known for his eloquence and proficiency in Latin and Greek. But he was best known as a Hebraist — an expert in Hebrew, the Old Testament, the Talmud and the Midrash. Certainly this man was not misguided by the English translation of the King James Bible. [*Cyclopedia of Biblical, Theological and Ecclesiastical Literature*, pp. 426-427]

Archbishop James Ussher was also a distinguished theologian, *"recognized as one of the greatest scholars of his time."* He was one of only six theologians allowed to address the Parliament and the King. *The Evangelical Dictionary of Theology* states, *"He was much sought after by contemporaries for his knowledge and beauty of character, and his personal impact was probably even greater than his scholarly legacy."* [*The Evangelical Dictionary of Theology*, p. 1131]

It is ironic that Dr. Ross, a man with little or no formal training in Bible languages, questions the Hebrew scholarship of these two great Christian educators. It is even harder to imagine why Ross would propose that these men were misguided by their reading of the King James Version Bible since both studied (and were published) almost exclusively in Latin — the language of scholarship of their day. The King James Version Bible was written in English.

CLAIM: Young-earth creationists are "Ussherites."

With full-knowledge that *"many young-earth creationists react to being labeled as 'Ussherites,'"* Creation and Time proceeds to apply this term to them in a derogatory manner. [p. 26] Dr. Ross further states that *"most scientists see little need to distinguish between Ussherite and non-Ussherite young-earthers. From these scientists' perspective, stretching the 6,000 years to 50,000 is inconsequential and does nothing to enhance credibility."* [p. 26] Therefore, in Ross's mind apparently, all young-earth creationists are "Ussherites" and without credibility.

FALSE. It is doubtful that any modern young-earth creation scientist or leader fully accepts Ussher's exact chronology. It is true that Bishop Ussher believed that Creation took place during 6 normal 24 hour days, approximately 6,000 years ago. To accept an approximate 6,000 year date does not make one an "Ussherite." This has been the view held by the majority of Christians and Jews throughout history — long before Ussher.

Anyone who is active in evangelism knows
that the issue of pain and suffering is a frequent obstacle.
People blame God for it,
and question Christianity's claim that God is love.

In recounting the history of the interpretation of the Creation days, it seems extraordinary that Dr. Ross has completely skipped over the views of the Reformers (approximately 100 years prior to Ussher's efforts). In studying these views, he would have noticed that such great biblical scholars as Luther and Calvin taught that the world was very young. Luther, for instance, stated *"we know from Moses that the world was not in existence before 6,000 years ago."* He insisted that Moses wrote about Creation in normal, literal language, *"he calls 'a spade a spade,' i.e., he employs the terms 'day' and 'evening' without allegory, just as we customarily do... we assert that Moses spoke in the literal sense, not allegorically or figuratively, i.e., that the world, with all its creatures, was created within six days, as the words read. If we do not comprehend the reason for this, let us remain pupils and leave the job of teacher to the Holy Spirit."* [Jaroslav Peliken, editor, "Luther's Works," *Lectures on Genesis Chapters 1-5,* Vol. 1 (St. Louis: Concordia Publishing House, 1958), pp. 3, 6]

The thing that makes Ussher's views distinct from the views of his predecessors is his attempt to give a precise point in time for the Creation event. Since most young-earth creationists do not believe a specific Creation date can be ascertained, it is not correct to use the term "Ussherite." Dr. Ross has used a broad brush to unfairly ridicule Christian brothers.

CLAIM: God would naturally take billions of years for Creation because He is a master craftsman.

Dr. Ross illustrates his belief that Creation took billions of years, *"Observe skilled sculptors, painters, or poets, artisans of any kind, and see that they always spend much more time on their masterpieces than they do on their ordinary tasks. Observe the painstaking yet joyful labor poured into each masterpiece of their design. Observe how often the artist stops to appreciate and evaluate the work in progress."* [p. 142]

FALSE. This type of reasoning is obviously in error. One must always be careful not to compare God to mankind, a mere shadow of deity. Would Dr. Ross lead us to believe that when Christ returns to create a new heaven and a new earth (a masterpiece beyond imagination) that this process will also take billions of years? God is unaffected by the limits of time. He may do it instantly. Or He may recreate it in six literal days.

Dr. Ross's illustration fails on both the divine and the human level. Although many masterpieces have taken years to finish, history is filled with accounts of artists, musicians and poets that were so inspired that their greatest endeavors took only days or weeks to complete. For example, Handel's entire masterpiece, "The Messiah," was written in just three weeks (August 22 to September 14, 1741). The lesson we learn is that the time it takes a craftsman to produce a masterpiece often depends upon his vision, ability and desire. The all-knowing God would not need billions of years of "fine-tuning" to produce His masterpiece. Of God's creative power, Psalm 33:9 states *"For He spoke, and it was done; He commanded, and it stood fast"* (NASB, NKJV).

More on Progressive Creationism's Billions-of-Years

CLAIM: Science has conclusively proven earth is old.

Chapter 9 of *Creation and Time* attempts to demonstrate that the age of the universe has been determined beyond any reasonable doubt. It further states that to reject the old universe date for Creation is equal to rejecting all of science and therefore separating our minds from our faith.

FALSE. There is no scientific method available to mortal humans that can positively prove the earth is very old — or very young, for that matter.

It would be wise to count the number of *assumptions* utilized in chapter 9 to reach the *conclusions* listed by Dr. Ross as scientific *fact*. Although young-earth creationists may not have verifiable answers for all the astrophysical phenomena mentioned in this chapter, they are working on it. And it is very important to recognize that scientific interpretations are not the same as scientific fact. History has demonstrated this point time and again.

In the context of this report, which focuses on Bible interpretation, Hebrew, and theology, it is not our purpose to deal with the technical, scientific issues involved. It is our understanding that at least four scientists, and perhaps more, are preparing scientific critiques on the various scientific claims made in *Creation and Time*. We leave the task in their able hands. For now, let it simply be said that answers already exist to some of the problems put forth by Dr. Ross. Other interesting scientific theories are in development.

Chapter 10 of *Creation and Time* surveys 10 evidences sometimes used by young-earth creationists to support a young universe. It attempts to persuade the reader that these evidences are actually wonderful indicators of an <u>old</u> universe when properly interpreted. It says that all of these evidences, *"when investigated closely, involve one or more of these four problems: Faulty assumptions, Faulty data, Misapplication of principles, laws, and equations, Failure to consider opposing evidence."* [p. 103]

The four problems listed are not solely associated with young-earth creationism. It is hardly necessary to state that those same charges could (and should) be leveled against Ross's interpretation of scientific data.

While it is not practical in this short summary to evaluate *Creation and Time's* treatment of each of the 10 evidences, the following examples should serve as a barometer of his methods:

Radiohalos

Pages 108-110 discuss Dr. Robert Gentry's discovery of granite crystal halos caused from the decay of Polonium 218. Dr. Gentry refers to these halos as God's fingerprints because he is convinced they are evidence for a young earth. Whatever one believes about this evidence, it is clear that *Creation and Time* has not played fair in this discussion. It references a geologist who insists that Dr. Gentry is incorrect about the type of rocks in which the halos were found. The book also quotes from scientists (Drs. Odom and Rink) who claim that halos can be formed by ultra-slow processes and thus Dr. Gentry's discovery actually proves an old-earth. After reading *Creation and Time's* analysis of this scientific information, any person might be tempted to agree that Gentry's evidences for a young earth are in error. When further research is done, however, it becomes apparent that Dr. Ross has not recorded the full story.

In fact, the *geologist* that has reported the errors of Dr. Gentry is a fireman and amateur geologist. One of the primary resources from which his testimony was noted by Dr. Ross is the magazine *Creation/Evolution*. This is a vehemently pro-evolution, anti-creationist journal and hardly an unbiased source. Furthermore, Dr. Gentry's book, *Creation's Tiny Mystery*, provides answers to Mr. Wakefield's charges and lists nearly 4 pages of errors reported in the *Creation/Evolution* article.

Additionally, it is significant that *Creation and Time* assures the readers that Drs. Odom and Rink have disproved Dr. Gentry. This is not the case, as even Dr. Odom admits. In a personal correspondence to Gentry, Dr. Odom writes, *"The science paper was the result of an accidental finding; it is not something that we are really working on. As is obvious in the paper, we have proven nothing - simply offered an alternative explanation. We had included a question mark at the end of our title of the paper, but it was removed apparently by the editor."* [emphasis added]

Not taking into account Dr. Gentry's response to these scientific objections means that Dr. Ross has fallen victim to one of his four stated scientific problems: *"Failure to consider opposing evidence."*

Earth's magnetic field

Another example of Ross's one-sided treatment of "young-earth" evidences is demonstrated on page 106, entitled *"The earth's magnetic field is decaying too rapidly."* *Creation and Time* cites Dr. Thomas Barnes's earlier view that reversals of the earth's magnetic field never happened, and then Ross refutes that view. However, during the late 1980's, most creationist scientists began to realize that the evidence for past reversals is overwhelming and Dr. Barnes's theories were reexamined. Dr. Russell Humphreys has developed a revised model for magnetic reversals, now widely accepted by young-earth creationists, which handles all the data and is based on sound principles of physics. Dr. Humphreys has demonstrated that the decay of the earth's magnetic field, in accordance with field reversal, is evidence for a young earth. [For a good summary of this evidence see: Dr. John D. Morris, *The Young Earth* (Colorado Springs, CO: Master Books, 1994), pp. 80-83]

The question that we would like to address is not whether this evidence is valid proof for a young earth (although it certainly seems to be), but whether or not Dr. Ross has presented young-earth evidences faithfully? The point is this, that Dr. Ross has cited outdated theories without even alluding to the fact that these theories have been rejected in favor of revised models. Dr. Ross knew about the more recent view of reversals and yet ignored it in his book. On June 9, 1991, Dr. Humphreys mailed Dr. Ross copies of his technical papers on geomagnetic reversals. In a letter to Dr. Humphreys, dated July 17, 1991, Dr. Ross acknowledged receiving those papers and implied that he had read them. The question must be asked, if Dr. Ross knew about Dr. Humphreys' revised model, why didn't he acknowledge this fact in *Creation in Time*? Why continue to "destroy" theories which are no longer widely held by young-earth creationists? It seems that once again Dr. Ross has fallen victim to two of his four stated scientific problems: *"Failure to consider opposing evidence, and working with faulty data."*

Once again we see the truth that although all scientists have the same evidences from nature, their interpretation of that data is often dependent upon foundational assumptions and presuppositions. One may well wonder if Dr. Ross is demonstrating that he has a blinding bias concerning the age of the universe.

CLAIM: The universe has to be billions of years old, otherwise life could not exist.

In a section entitled "The Narrow Window of Time," *Creation and Time* suggests that a universe, galaxy, star, planet and moon must all be the precise right age for life to exist. Dr. Ross claims that this age must be in the billions of years. *"Also ruled out is a time scale for the universe and the earth of only a few thousand years, for all five of the relevant bodies must be at least a billion years old (recognizing that*

God does not create with appearance of age) to be ready for life." [p. 138]

FALSE. It is dangerous to teach that God <u>could not</u> create a universe, galaxy, and planet that could support life in a short period of time. God could do it in an instant!

If God's goal was to produce a suitable living environment for Man, could He create it with a word of His mouth? Of course! And if God did this miracle (as stated in the Bible), yet fallen humans have somehow misinterpreted nature because of their incorrect bias, can God rightly be accused of being deceptive?

Creation and Time condemns the premise of creation having *any* appearance of age. Yet, is it scientific to try to measure the age of something we know did not occur naturally? A simple reading of Scripture insists that the world was created mature. God is not deceptive; He tells us this fact in the first chapter of His Word. Let us not accuse God because we choose the measuring stick of this present generation rather than the canon of Scripture.

CLAIM: God used the Big Bang to create the universe.

Dr. Ross claims that the universe began with a God-engineered Big Bang about 17 billion years ago, plus or minus 3 billion years. He claims that the Big Bang Theory has been "undeniably" proven. [*Creation and Time*, pp. 91-118, 129; *Fingerprint of God*, pp. 158-159; Hugh Ross, "Why Big Bang Opponents Never Say Die," *Facts & Faith newsletter*, Vol. 4, No. 4 (Winter 1990-91)]

Is the Big Bang really an undeniable, proven fact? Astronomer Halton Arp has written, *"Cosmology is unique in science in that it is a vary large intellectual edifice based on very few facts."* [Halton C. Arp, et. al., "*The Extragalactic Universe; An Alternative view,*" *Nature*, Vol. 346 (August 30, 1990), pp. 807-812] Sir Fred Hoyle, a famous British astronomer and cosmologist has stated, *"the main efforts of investigators have been in papering over holes in the big bang theory, to build up an idea that has become ever more complex and cumber-*

some... I have little hesitation in saying that a sickly pall now hangs over the big bang theory." [Fred Hoyle, *"The Big Bang Under Attack," Science Digest,* Vol. 92 (May 1984), p. 84]

One wonders what would happen to Dr. Ross's understanding of creationism if one day the world community of scientists join the secular dissenters and decide that the Big Bang really is nothing more than a "big bust." He has taught the Big Bang theory so strongly that if it is ever abandoned by the majority of scientists, as one day may be the case, it will be a major embarrassment to his ministry.

Dr. Ross's repeated and emphatic claim throughout his writings and talks that the universe is 17 billion years old, plus or minus 3 billion years is also a dangerous stand. (e.g., p. 101) In our experience, more knowledgeable old-earth scientists acknowledge that the claimed age estimate for the universe will continue to vary in the future as it has in the past. At this moment, leading experts are using 14 billion to 9 billion years as their best estimate. While other calculations indicate it could be as young as 7 billion years. [See 1994 issues of *Nature* and *The Astrophysical Journal*] New instruments, future observations and new methods and theories will certainly change this and every other figure. As NASA's Steve Maran recently said, anyone who thinks that this issue is settled *"has been looking through their telescope too long."* ["Scientists' Report Narrow Gap in Estimated Age of the Universe" (Gannett News Service, September 29, 1994)]

Denouncing Young-Earth Creationists

An affinity for secular evolutionists over young-earth Christians

Chapter 4, entitled "The *Winds of War*," discusses the history of creation/evolution debates from Darwin until the present. It is noteworthy that evolutionists are consistently given more respect than the young-earth creationists. Amazingly, the book seems to suggest that young-earth creationists are causing a lot of hurt and trouble in this world, perhaps even more than evolutionists.

This chapter further reveals Dr. Ross's bias against young-earth creationists, whom he considers to be unscientific and foolish. From his writings, it is reasonable to believe that he feels more affinity with secular scientists than with his Christian brothers who believe in a recent Creation. This is despite Ross's cries for tolerance on such a "trivial matter."

CLAIM: The motivation of young-earth creationists is fear.

According to *Creation and Time*, young-earth creationists are motivated by fear. They are afraid that Darwinian evolution could occur given enough time. *"History reveals, however, the driving force behind this theological artifice (young earth creationism): It is fear rather than fact. Fear says long creation days somehow accommodate the Dar-*

winian claim that by strictly natural processes operating over four bil-
lion years, life arose from a primordial soup and evolved on its own
into human beings." [p. 72]

Dr. Ross explores this question further in Chapter 7. He states that young-earth creationists are led to deny long Creation days because they actually fear that evolution could occur if enough time is permitted. He feels that this is ironic; that young-earthers actually have a stronger belief in evolution than he does.

> FALSE. Dr. Ross is sadly and laughably incorrect if he really believes that young-earth creationists are driven by fear of evolution. Few, if any, theologians who believe in Progressive Creation would make this type of statement. In reality, Dr. Ross owes a debt to young-earth creationists. They developed many of the arguments which he now uses to fight against evolutionism. No, young-earth creationists are not fearful of the possibility of evolution. They are fearful of the destruction evolutionism and a secular worldview is causing in society due to its anti-God, anti-Bible belief system. Young-earth creationists are distressed to see so many Christians repeating the same cycle of mistakes experienced in the past — errors that caused so many to lose faith in God's Word — blunders that hurt the effectiveness of the Church.

Young-earth creationists are distressed to see
so many Christians repeating the same cycle of
mistakes experienced in the past — errors that
caused so many to lose faith in God's Word —
blunders that hurt the effectiveness of the Church.

Chapter 7 of *Creation and Time* seems to show that Dr. Ross does not fully understand this issue. Evolution is a scientific impossibility whether we assume the age of the universe is 6,000 or 600 billion years. Young-earth creationists take their theological stand on this issue because the Bible clearly indicates that earth is only thousands of years old and because to claim otherwise is destructive to the gospel.

CLAIM: Young-earth creationists have no scientific support; they are operating on blind faith.

Creation and Time accuses young-universe creationists of claiming scientific support, *"knowing that it does not exist outside their own circle."* [p. 118] Dr. Ross bemoans what it must be like to be a young-earth creationist, *"I'm saddened to think of what living with this tension must be like, especially as I recall the old adage, 'The heart cannot rejoice in what the mind rejects.'"* [p. 118]

FALSE. There is a great deal of scientific evidence in favor of young-earth, biblical creationism. [See "For Further Information" section for a sampling of works offering scientific evidences] Dr. Ross may rest assured that young-universe hearts are rejoicing all around the world. Anyone who has been involved in Creation evangelism can testify to the joy experienced by those who have been enlightened. A heavy burden of confusion has been lifted from their shoulders. God's truth brightens their minds and hearts.

We cannot help but recall another old saying, *"See to it that no one takes you captive through philosophy and empty deception, according to the tradition of men, according to the elementary principles of the world, rather than according to Christ"* (Colossians 2:8).

Ross: *"Young-universe creationists convince many whose science education and biblical training are insufficient to evaluate the evidence."* [p. 103]

Of course, many who are persuaded to accept Dr. Ross's perspective also lack Bible and science training. Such a statement proves little or nothing.

Anyone involved in the creation science movement is familiar with the many fine scientists with doctoral and master's degrees from prestigious institutions of higher learning. Many of these scientists have had long careers in research positions and/or professorships. They are true men and women of science, critical thinkers and scholars. Many of the people we have seen join the young-earth creation ranks have been science buffs or science professionals. Ross's statement smacks of a back-handed attack against any and all would-be young-earth creationists. One may wonder if he is trying to intimidate those readers who are as yet undecided about this issue.

Judging by the arrogance of these claims, the irony here is that Dr. Ross apparently considers himself an adept interpretator of the Bible and Hebrew (fields in which he has little or no formal training) and seemingly qualified to judge many disciplines of science (in which he has little or no formal training).

CLAIM: Young-universe creationists deny physical reality, and they are arrogant, too.

Chapter 11 of *Creation and Time* paints a picture of young-universe creationists as people who are centuries behind the times and who even deny physical reality. *"Few Christians are yet aware of the anti-physical tendency within young-universe creationism."* [p. 122]

Dr. Ross goes on to compare those who believe in recent Creation with: (a) the church who persecuted Galileo, (b) the ungodly parents of the man Jesus cured from congenital blindness, and (c) the early Gnostic heretics. He warns that this attitude continues to spawn heresies in modern times, *"I believe there's a need for alertness within the camp of Christian orthodoxy to the encroachment of anti-physical notions."* [p. 122]

He states that this *"denial of physical reality"* doesn't occur only in areas of origin science but *"even events taking place in the present are denied."* [p. 122] Ross admonishes the reader that *"a sound mind accepts reality, physical and spiritual, not to mention emotional."* [p. 124]

More than a little contempt is shown by the following quote in which Ross presumes to speak for the young-universe creationist: *"Evangelical or fundamentalist scientists who disagree with the young-universe creationists' view can be ignored or discredited."* *Creation and Time* continues with its assessment, *"Some young-earth creationists see themselves as having a corner on truth about the cosmos."* [p. 123]

FALSE. It is absurd to say that young-earth creation scientists deny physical reality. Based on some of Ross's scientific and biblical claims, it appears they are more aware of "physical reality" than Dr. Ross. These scientists have spent their life in the study and pursuit of physical reality — the true, physical facts about our earth and universe. How can Dr. Ross claim that *scientists* using *scientific* information are denying reality? It seems that he is upset that these scientists are denying his version of reality.

Further, to wrongly compare young-earth creationists to the heretics of all ages does not show the "love and compassion" of the moral high-ground Ross attempts to take early on in his book. One gets the impression that Dr. Ross is indeed writing from the very depths of hurt feelings, wearing his injuries on his sleeve in a very unflattering manner.

In trying to show that young-earth creationists deny reality, *Creation and Time* states, *"Even events taking place in the present are denied. Many young-universe creationists claim that star formation is one of God's miracles of creation and, therefore, could take place only during the appropriate Genesis creation day."* [p. 122]

MISLEADING. *Creation and Time* lists 6 references in support of this claim. After reading each of these resources one finds that half never address the question of *when* the stars were formed, except that they could not have been formed by the Big Bang. Five of the six give *scientific* evidence that star formation cannot be explained by the Big Bang model. Once again Dr. Ross has misrepresented his references.

CLAIM: Young-earth creationists are divisive.

Creation and Time paints a picture of young-earth creationists dividing the church and causing great harm. In fact, it equates them with the "circumcision party" of Paul's time that insisted that all Gentile converts must become Jewish prior to being Christian. The council of Jerusalem made it clear that circumcision was not required for salvation. Still the Jewish sympathizers followed the apostles and caused trouble in many Gentile communities.

Ross states, *"Much as circumcision divided the first-century church, I see the creation date issue dividing the church of this century. As circumcision distorted the gospel and hampered evangelism, so, too, does young-universe creationism."* [p. 162]

FALSE. Although rare individuals within any movement may have a divisive attitude, this is certainly not the character of the young-earth creation movement. These men and women are not proposing some new and far-out theory; they are holding to the position of historic Christianity. It seems to us that it is Progressive Creationism that has stepped away from the historic Judeo-Christian position.

Once again, we know of no creationist who makes belief in a young-earth a requirement for salvation. Further, it is offensive to see Dr. Ross compare young-earth creationists to ungodly characters in the Bible and church history. In fact, this claim seems ironic considering the fact that young-earth creationism has been the historic position of the church since the time of the apostles. Ross has not provided any persuasive evidence for his insinuation that young-earth creationists *"distort the gospel and hamper evangelism."* [p. 162]

Young-earth creation ministries have been formed all over the world for the express purpose of evangelization. We realize that one way of introducing people to Jesus Christ is to help them understand the love He showed in His act of creation. In *The Roots of Evil*, John Wenham states, *"Evil constitutes the biggest single argument against the existence of an almighty, loving God. At the same time its study provides the most direct route to an understanding of the way the universe is run. The subject is crucial to those who are searching for truth and wishing to grapple with the claims of Christianity, and to Christians who wish to deepen their grasp and come to grips with their doubts."* [John W. Wenham in Norman L. Geisler, *The Roots of Evil* (Grand Rapids, MI: Zondervan Publishing, 1979), p. 89.]

Although Dr. Ross does attempt to answer the problem of evil and suffering in this world, his answer is terribly unsatisfying. He denies original paradise and downplays the suffering of animals and man (animals don't really suffer, and man's suffering is only for a short time). In reality, people need to understand that God created a wonderful paradise and that suffering, death and evil came into the world through Adam's sin. Dr. Geisler points out, "It *was man who brought the fall to the world (brought evil into the world), he can work to remove the effects of that fall (i.e., suffering) without being concerned about fighting against God.*" [Norman L. Geisler, *The Roots of Evil* (Grand Rapids, MI: Zondervan Publishing, 1979), p. 68] Those who spread the good news of God's recent, loving, Creation are not hampering evangelism, they are helping to bring understanding to the world, bringing glory to the Creator.

CLAIM: The Bible-Science Association said that Hugh Ross rejects Christ's Atonement.

Creation and Time states that the BSA falsely accused him by "*claiming that I reject Christ's atonement.*" [p. 83]

FALSE. Here is what the BSA actually said: "Ross's version of earth history rejects the connection that Scripture establishes between sin, death and Christ's atonement."

This statement does not say what *Creation and Time* claims. It simply states the true beliefs of Dr. Ross — that he rejects a theological link between sin, physical death and Christ's atonement. Dr. Ross's representation of the article seems to be an attempt to show that he is a martyr at the hands of young-earth creationist ministries. This is not a true sentiment.

CLAIM: Young-earth creationists say salvation depends on belief in 24-hour-days and recent Creation.

Creation and Time teaches that young-earth creationists "*carry another torch, upholding twenty-four-hour creation days and recent creation dates as essential requirements for salvation.*" [p. 84]

FALSE. Once again Dr. Ross seems to depict himself as a martyr of dogma — and young-earth creationists as blind and misguided.

Nowhere, however, has Dr. Ross shown that young-earth creationists teach that adherence to the belief in twenty-four-hour Creation days is a requirement for salvation. The young-earth creationists' quotes referred to in *Creation and Time* unanimously voice concern that Progressive Creationism is a corruption of biblical theology and doctrine.

CLAIM: Wendell Bird "is not committed" to a young universe.

Reference no. 7 of chapter 11 (concerning Attorney W.R. Bird, *The Origin of Species Revisited*): *"Though these volumes support a young-universe interpretation, in a recent personal communication, Wendell Bird made it clear that he is not committed to the young-universe cause."* [p. 177]

FALSE. Wendell Bird is a creationist well-known for arguing a creation science case before the U.S. Supreme Court. *Creation and Time* gives the impression that he is not a young-earth creationist.

We faxed this part of *Creation and Time* to Mr. Bird. His response: *"Both statements in Hugh Ross's footnotes are incorrect, and simply garbled. I remain, as I have been, a young-earth creationist."* Bird also said that Ross is incorrect when he claims that *The Origin of Species Revisited* supports a young-universe interpretation. Bird purposely did not address that issue. Due to the nature of his ministry within the creation ministry, although Bird is a young-earth creationist, he does not *"take a public position on the issue at all, and focuses instead on origin events."* [personal communication from attorney Wendell Bird, June 11, 1994]

Conclusion

Dr. D. James Kennedy's popular book, *What if Jesus Had Never Been Born?* notes, *"Calvin said that the Bible — God's special revelation — was spectacles that we must put on if we are to correctly read the book of nature — God's revelation in creation. Unfortunately, between the beginning of science and our day, many scientists have discarded these glasses, and many distortions have followed."* [D. James Kennedy and Jerry Newcombe, *What if Jesus Had Never Been Born?* (Nashville, Tennessee: Thomas Nelson, Inc., Publishers, 1994), p. 102] In contrast, Dr. Ross clearly believes that we must put on the eyeglasses of modern science if we are to fully understand the Bible. Dr. Ross's view of the relationship between special and general revelation stands in complete and total opposition to that of John Calvin, one of the most influential theologians of all time.

Sound interpretations of the Bible (built upon a literal, historical, grammatical hermeneutic) should not be invalidated by the ever-changing whims of secular origins science. Although science is a good and valuable thing, we must keep our eyes open and remain on guard to the lies and distortions of men. Due to human depravity, the "facts" of science can be misrepresented; even the experimentation of man can be twisted to sinful ends. True scientific facts will always complement God's Word. Although man has the ability to twist even the Word of God, we can conclude from reliable historic study that the position of the church, from the time of the apostles, has been that the Creation event occurred in six literal days only a few thousand years ago.

It is not a joyful thing to write a critique of another man's work. Had this matter not seemed so important, we would certainly rather have directed our energies toward other, less burdensome matters. We pray for the day when Dr. Ross will improve his presentations toward better biblical and scientific accuracy. In that day, we trust the Lord will expand the fruitfulness of his ministry.

We pray that Progressive Creationists will come to realize that recent Creation is not a trivial belief; it is foundational, as John Calvin understood. Calvin realized that many of the most important theological truths are often ridiculed, yet he stood strong, knowing that the Church must not stop teaching these truths:

> *"They will not refrain from guffaws when they are informed that but <u>little more than five thousand years have passed since the creation of the universe</u>... Must we pass over in silence the creation of the universe? No! God's truth is so powerful, both in this respect and in every other, that it has nothing to fear from the evil speaking of wicked men."* [John Calvin, The Institutes of the Christian Religion — emphasis added]

Christians must not fall into the trap of dismissing such an important theme as merely a matter of one's conscience or a side-issue to be avoided in polite company. It is hoped this report will challenge readers to investigate the Bible for themselves, using sound hermeneutic processes. As Christians, we must be willing to place our faith in the sure words of Scripture, over and above all other claims of truth. We may not have all the scientific explanations for natural phenomenon, but good research is currently being accomplished. While questions remain, we take our stand for God's Word, which we find to be explicitly clear on this issue.

Hebrews indicates that our Creator is pleased when we accept His account of Creation by faith. *"<u>By faith</u> we understand that the universe was formed at God's command, so that what is seen was not made out of what was visible... And <u>without faith it is impossible to please God</u>, because anyone who comes to him must believe that he exists and that he rewards those who earnestly seek him"* (Hebrews 11:3,6, *NIV*). We must trust the information that God has provided. We must stand firm upon the foundation of His written revelation. In this, the believer finds great joy and satisfaction, knowing that we are true to our Lord.

For Further Information

(in alphabetical order)

Answers Book: Answers to the 12 Most-Asked Questions on Genesis and Creation/Evolution, Revised Edition, by Ken Ham, Dr. Andrew Snelling and Dr. Carl Wieland (Colorado Springs, Colorado: Master Books, 1991), 208 pp.

Astronomy and the Bible by Dr. Donald B. DeYoung (Grand Rapids, Michigan: Baker Book House, 1989), 146 pp.

Bible and Astronomy by Dr. John C. Whitcomb (Winona Lake, Indiana: BMH Books, 1984), 32 pp.

Biblical Basis for Modern Science by Dr. Henry M. Morris (Grand Rapids, Michigan: Baker Book House, 1984), 516 pp.

Biblical Creationism: What Each Book of the Bible Teaches about Creation and the Flood by Dr. Henry M. Morris (Grand Rapids, Michigan: Baker Book House, 1993), 276 pp.

Controversy: Roots of the Creation-Evolution Conflict by Dr. Donald E. Chittick (Portland, Oregon: Multnomah Press, 1984), 280 pp.

Creation Research Society Quarterly (P.O. Box 969, Ashland, Ohio 44805-0969).

Creation: Ex Nihilo magazine, Phone 1-800-350-3232 (USA).

Early Earth, Revised Edition, by Dr. John C. Whitcomb (Grand Rapids, MI: Baker Book House, 1986), 174 pp.

Genesis and the Decay of the Nations by Ken Ham (Brisbane: Creation Science Foundation; Colorado Springs, Colorado: Master Books, 1991), 81 pp.

Genesis Record: A Scientific and Devotional Commentary on the Book of Beginnings by Dr. Henry M. Morris (Grand Rapids, Michigan: Baker Book House, 1976), 716 pp.

Genesis Solution by Ken Ham and Paul S. Taylor (Grand Rapids, Michigan: Baker Book House, 1988), 126 pp.

History of Modern Creationism by Dr. Henry M. Morris (Colorado Springs, Colorado: Master Books, 1984), 382 pp.

Illustrated ORIGINS Answer Book, Fourth Edition, by Paul S. Taylor (Mesa, Arizona: Eden Productions, an imprint of Films for Christ, 1993), 128 pp. (Ph. 602/894-0445).

In the Minds of Men: Darwin and the New World Order by Ian T. Taylor (Toronto: TFE Publishing, 1984), 498 pp.

King of Creation by Dr. Henry M. Morris (Colorado Springs, Colorado: Master Books, 1980), 239 pp.

ORIGINS: How the World Came to Be (six 30-minute films/videos that reveal an intriguing summary of evidence for Creation and against evolutionism) directed by Paul S. Taylor and Jan Bodzinga (Mesa, Arizona: Eden Productions/Films for Christ, 1982), Phone 602/894-1300.

Science, Scripture, and the Young Earth: An Answer to the Current Attacks on the Biblical Doctrines of Recent Creation and the Global Flood by Dr. Henry M. Morris and Dr. John D. Morris (El Cajon, California: Institute for Creation Research, 1989), 95 pp.

The Young Earth by Dr. John D. Morris (Colorado Springs, CO: Master Books, 1994), 220 pp.

Index

About the authors

Mark Van Bebber received his Masters of Divinity degree with highest honors from Western Theological Seminary (now Phoenix Seminary) of Arizona. He received his B.A. in Biblical Studies (graduating with highest honors and several academic awards) from Arizona College of the Bible where he currently serves on the part-time teaching faculty. Mark is the director of ministry outreach and customer relations for Films for Christ. He and his wife, Beth, have two children, Christian and Alexandra.

Paul S. Taylor has been involved in creationist research and media production for over 25 years and is currently the Executive Director of Films for Christ, an interdenominational Christian film and literature ministry. He is concerned that few young people have a firm understanding of the foundations of Christianity and history found in Genesis, the book of beginnings. To this end, he has authored various popular creationist articles and books, including *The Illustrated ORIGINS Answer Book* and *The Great Dinosaur Mystery and the Bible*. Paul has directed various award-winning motion pictures including *The World That Perished*, *ORIGINS: How the World Came to Be*, and *The Genesis Solution*. He and his wife, Star, have four children: Heather, Eric, Laura and Andrew.

To obtain a free catalog of other faith-strengthening books and videos offered by Films for Christ/Eden Productions, write or call:

Films for Christ
2628 West Birchwood Circle
Mesa, Arizona 85202
Phone: 800-332-2261 or 602-894-1300
EMail: 71742.2074@compuserve.com